Democracy's Dangers & Discontents

*The Hoover Institution gratefully acknowledges
the following individuals and foundations
for their significant support of the*
WORKING GROUP ON THE ROLE OF MILITARY
HISTORY IN CONTEMPORARY CONFLICT

VICTOR AND KAREN TRIONE

WILLARD AND MARGARET CARR

THE LYNDE AND HARRY BRADLEY FOUNDATION

Democracy's Dangers & Discontents

The Tyranny of the Majority from the Greeks to Obama

Bruce S. Thornton

HOOVER INSTITUTION PRESS

STANFORD UNIVERSITY   STANFORD, CALIFORNIA

The Hoover Institution on War, Revolution and Peace, founded at Stanford University in 1919 by Herbert Hoover, who went on to become the thirty-first president of the United States, is an interdisciplinary research center for advanced study on domestic and international affairs. The views expressed in its publications are entirely those of the authors and do not necessarily reflect the views of the staff, officers, or Board of Overseers of the Hoover Institution.

www.hoover.org

Hoover Institution Press Publication No. 653

Hoover Institution at Leland Stanford Junior University,
Stanford, California 94305-6010

First printing 2014
20 19 18 17 16 15 14   7 6 5 4 3 2 1

Manufactured in the United States of America

The paper used in this publication meets the minimum Requirements
of the American National Standard for Information Sciences—
Permanence of Paper for Printed Library Materials, ANSI/NISO
Z39.48-1992. ⊚

Cataloging-in-Publication Data is available from
the Library of Congress.
ISBN: 978-0-8179-1794-4 (cloth. : alk. paper)
ISBN: 978-0-8179-1796-8 (epub)
ISBN: 978-0-8179-1797-5 (mobi)
ISBN: 978-0-8179-1798-2 (PDF)

For Esau Kane Thornton
At tibi prima, puer, munuscula

CONTENTS

FOREWORD

Bruce Thornton has written a number of books about the history and nature of democratic government, past and present, especially the dangerous tendency of majority-rule societies to embrace a therapeutic mindset rather than to accept the tragic limitations of the human condition (*Plagues of the Mind: The New Epidemic of False Knowledge*).

Thornton sees limited, republican government as the salvation of civilized societies, but he has also warned that through affluence and license consensual societies can ossify into self-gratification and indifference to their own long-term health and viability (*Decline and Fall: Europe's Slow Motion Suicide*, written well before the European Union financial crisis).

In the recent *The Wages of Appeasement: Ancient Athens, Munich, and Obama's America*, Thornton turned to complacent democracies' unfortunate habit of shorting defense spending and finding themselves unable to deter aggressive and authoritarian states. Now, in *Democracy's Danger and Discontents: The Tyranny of the Majority from the Greeks to Obama*, Thornton has combined those prior investigations of democratic maladies, both their internal and external affairs, into a comprehensive explanation of the cause of these disturbing symptoms of majority rule. What follows is a 2,500-year annotated exploration about why and how democracies seem to implode—and the correctives for their excesses offered by brilliant ancient and modern observers.

There are plenty of examples of democratic excess—and dire warnings about it—in the life and thought of Western civilization. Thucydides's wartime Athenians ordered the execution of all the Mytileneans one day, and not quite all of them the next. Plato abhorred rule by the majority. The trajectory of Jean-Jacques Rousseau's call to arms that "man is born free, and everywhere he is in chains" ended with the French Revolution's *Comité de salut public*. Alexis de Tocqueville hoped that perhaps America's unique homestead farmer and an autonomous middle class might check the passions on a fickle underclass. *Democracy's Danger and Discontents* adds lots more examples of democracy's strengths but also its myriad excesses. Whereas faces change, causes come and go, crises appear and reappear, the problems of radically democratic societies stay the same. Why do such governments, so ideal in theory, so often—to borrow an earlier Thornton phrase—commit slow-motion suicide in fact?

Most of what modern egalitarians chafe at in our own system of government—the Electoral College, the allotment of two senators per state regardless of population size, the Second Amendment—are the constitutional remnants of the Founding Fathers' worries that a *demos* might degenerate into an *ochlos*, a veritable mob demanding that its always increasing appetites be met by the state. In contrast, republican government, representative government, and constitutional government were the Founders' solutions to square the circle of ensuring consent of the governed while protecting property, unpopular expression, and minority rights.

Bruce Thornton is also a research fellow at the Hoover Institution and a member of our Working Group on the Role of Military History in Contemporary Conflict, which seeks to make sense of contemporary national security issues in light of the history of the past. *Democracy's Danger and Discontents* repeatedly warns about the predictable populist hatred for the better off, the capricious nature of direct voting that was so often predicated on gifted speakers rousing the crowd to fury, and the inevitable lowering of standards to ensure the widest participation of the populace in civic and public life. That said, Thornton is most concerned about the consistent democratic tendency to short collective defense in favor of subsidies for the people. These indulgences, Thornton reminds us, can lead to a society that equates each drachma, sestertius, or euro invested in a hoplite, legionary, or NATO jet as one less devoted to ensuring free admission to the theater, a supplement to the daily grain dole, or a cost-of-living increase in a government pension.

The democratic desire to cut defense and expand redistributive payouts to the citizenry might explain why the descendants of the heroes of Salamis could not stop Philip of Macedon. The latter, like the Persians a century and a half earlier, invaded from the north, but this time successfully with an army only a tenth of the size that had failed under Xerxes. Rome of the fifth century AD—a million square miles, seventy million citizens—could not stop the onslaughts of motley tribes crossing the Rhine and Danube, though their far poorer and less numerous Republican ancestors defeated Hannibal, the greatest military genius of his age.

Thornton argues that nothing much has changed in the new twenty-first century. Yet he is even more worried that consumption and entitlements are now energized as never before by the advent of modernism and high technology, the former offering the rationale for spending what you do not have, the latter the means of even more addictive gratification.

In the high-tech, nuclear age, there is less margin of error than in the Athens of Cleon or the Rome of Caesar and Brutus. Shorting defense these days can lead to nuclear Armageddon, serial 9/11-like attacks, or the collapse of entire computer systems that run the United States. Providing expanded entitlements for tens of millions of Americans can lead to chronic $1 trillion deficits that end national security altogether— debts of a magnitude that might astonish even bread-and-circus Romans.

Cheap consumer goods and electronics mean that poverty is no longer Dickensian, given that the urban impoverished have more computing power in their readily accessible iPhones than did Silicon Valley aristocrats just ten years prior. The poor of Rome or Paris may have agitated for bread; today, American poverty is mostly a relative condition. It matters little whether today's high-tech entry-level Kia is accessible to the poor and a far better automobile than yesterday's top-of-the-line Mercedes—if some people still must settle for Kias while the 1 percent enjoy an updated and more impressive Mercedes.

Thornton warns of a world where standards always relax, rarely tighten, minimal responsibilities give way to greater rights, budgets grow more than shrink, and an intrusive state becomes all-intrusive. He also cautions that acknowledging these tendencies—and the brilliant critics of them—is not the same as curtailing them. The end of democratic society is reached not when petroleum is exhausted or soils depleted or the atmosphere artificially warmed, but when we reach a state of egalitarian ennui, and the passive citizen remains unconvinced that his own democracy is any better than the alternative. At that point the public purse is usually exhausted, and what were once minor challenges become existential obstacles that cannot be overcome.

Democracy's Danger and Discontents offers a spirited defense of constitutional government by warning that its enemies are more likely found within ourselves than abroad—and that being equal matters little if we are not first free and safe.

VICTOR DAVIS HANSON
Martin and Illie Anderson Senior Fellow, Classics/Military History
Chairman, Working Group on the Role of Military History
in Contemporary Conflict
Hoover Institution, Stanford University

ACKNOWLEDGMENTS

I owe a debt of gratitude to the hospitality and support of the Hoover Institution and the staff of the Hoover Institution Press; to the long friendship of Victor Davis Hanson; to the patience of Craig Bernthal, Mark Arvanigian, Terry Scambray, and Paul Kaser in listening to me think out loud about the topics of this book; and, as always, to my wife, Jacalyn, for her steadfast love and wifery.

INTRODUCTION

The Triumph of Democracy and the Antidemocratic Tradition

On Christmas Day 1991, the hammer-and-sickle of the USSR that had flown above the Kremlin for over seven decades was lowered and replaced by the tricolor flag of Russia. In those few moments the Soviet Union, the nuclear-armed communist superpower that had challenged and threatened the liberal democracies of the West, was left in the dustbin of history that its rulers had long predicted would be the fate of liberal democracy. For many, the end of the Cold War, which had been cast as a conflict between democratic freedom and totalitarian servitude, was more than just one nation's victory over an undemocratic regime and a repudiation of domestic challenges such as socialism or the antidemocratic New Left of the 1960s and '70s.

The victory over the Soviet Union was also the vindication of liberal democracy and freedom as the "single principle," as political philosopher Pierre Manent calls it, the universal political system most suited for the modern capitalist societies to which all the world's people presumably aspire.[1] In subsequent decades the expansion of democracies across the globe seemingly confirmed this optimism. According to Freedom House, in 1989, when the Eastern bloc broke from the Soviet Union and began its dissolution, there were 69 electoral democracies.

---

1. In *Democracy without Nations?*, trans. Paul Seaton (Wilmington, DE, 2007), 83.

Today, there are 117.[2] More recently, many greeted the "Arab Spring," the uprisings and revolutions that started in December 2010 in the Middle East, as yet another expansion of democracy and a sign of its inevitable triumph.

The disappearance of the last major challenge to democracy and the latter's apparent global expansion have enhanced democracy's prestige, giving it what historian Michael Mandelbaum calls the "the best of good names," a form of government "honored and valued everywhere" with "the same kind of aura that surrounds medicine," and esteemed as "a high human achievement that improves the lives of those fortunate enough to come into contact with it."[3] This universal reputation has culminated the two-century-long elevation of popular government into the only acceptable form of government, and democracy promotion a noble foreign policy goal, a belief still powerful in the twenty-first century despite the recent evidence that internationally democracy is in retreat, as Joshua Kurlantzick documents.[4]

Democracy indeed is an astonishing historical phenomenon. That political freedom and citizen equality, liberal democracy's most important goals, should have arisen at all in the city-states of ancient Greece of the eighth century BC is a remarkable occurrence. The notion that free citizens collectively rule and exercise autonomy over their lives based on laws, offices, and the distribution of power through neutral electoral procedures and public accountability is equally bizarre in the context of the other civilizations of antiquity. More typical was the pyramidal power-structures of empires such as Egypt or Persia, in which kings and tiny elites monopolized force and resources and ruled their societies as personal possessions—societies in which the mass of people were coerced, unfree subjects, in contrast to the self-governing free citizens of the Greek city-states.

---

2. "Freedom in the World 2012," http://www.freedomhouse.org/sites/default/files/inline_images/Electoral%20Democracy%20Numbers%20FIW%201989-2012–Draft_0.pdf.

3. In *Democracy's Good Name* (New York, 2007), 96.

4. In *Democracy in Retreat* (New Haven, CT, and London, 2013).

Yet democracy—the empowerment of all male citizens regardless of birth or wealth—was just one form of constitutional government invented by the ancient Greeks. And it was the one most criticized and feared even before the fall of Athenian democracy in the late fourth century BC seemingly confirmed democracy's fatal flaws. Indeed, until the early nineteenth century, as a form of government "democracy" was looked on as dangerously unstable, prone to violent upheaval, class warfare, and the redistribution of property that followed from endowing the mass of people, Alexander Hamilton's "great beast," with political power.[5]

From the perspective of the antidemocratic tradition, today's idealization of democracy is itself remarkable. This tradition began with the history of the world's first democracy, ancient Athens. The failures and excesses of the Athenians, particularly their oppressive imperial rule over other Greek cities, and their near-destruction after the Peloponnesian War with Sparta, seemingly validated the dangers of radical popular rule. This criticism set the tone for subsequent political philosophers, giving point to historian J. S. McClelland's observation, "It could almost be said that political theorizing was *invented* to show that democracy, the rule of men by themselves, necessarily turns into rule by the mob." Thus the tradition of Western political theory began with a "profoundly antidemocratic bias."[6] Any admiration of Athens was limited to its artistic, literary, and philosophical achievements, or the lives and deeds of a few historical figures like Solon, Themistocles, and Pericles—and even those heroes at times were tarnished by their involvement in the creation of Athenian democracy. When it came to practical government, for most political theorists the mixed constitutions of Sparta or Rome were considered better models, and for some even monarchy was preferred to democracy.

Despite this long antidemocratic tradition, seldom have today's champions of democracy acknowledged its complexities and flaws.

---

5. Attributed to Hamilton in *The Memoirs of Theophilus Parsons* (1859); in Henry Adams, *History of the United States of America during the Administrations of Jefferson and Madison*, abr. and ed. Ernest Samuels (Chicago and London, 1967), 65.

6. In *The Crowd and the Mob* (London and Boston, 1989), 1–2.

However, from the ancient Greeks to the framers of the US Constitution, that tradition raised numerous questions. Are the people wise or knowledgeable enough to be entrusted with political power? Can they resist the wiles and manipulations of demagogues? Can elected officials pursue the long-term good of the state when they are accountable to those who put them in office, and who often seek the gratification of their own short-term interests and passions? Do the verbal processes of deliberation and decision-making among a multitude of voters render democracy even more vulnerable to demagoguery? Will not the people use their political power and control of institutions to redistribute property from the rich to the poor? Can a democracy, focused as it is on the short-term interests of the people, and dependent on the decision-making of the many armed with the vote and able to hold politicians accountable, conduct foreign policy effectively? And finally, do not the political freedom and equality of opportunity pursued by democracy inevitably degenerate into appetitive license and radical egalitarianism, and create the demand that governmental power be used to satisfy both?

The American founders, schooled in this tradition, recognized all these dangers and sought to avoid them by creating the mixed government of the Constitution. The power of the people to elect directly their representatives was limited to the House of Representatives. The remaining officials, including senators, the president, and the Supreme Court, were elected indirectly to provide an institutional "filtering" that would temper the interests and passions of individuals and factions in order to find virtuous and wise leaders, and to check the power of the majority over the minority, and the power of elites over the majority. The innate hunger for power in all people, whether taken in the mass or in elites defined by wealth or birth, would then be held in check, their factional interests limiting each other, so that the federal government could not become the instrument of tyranny. And tyranny was the great fear of democracy's critics going back to the ancient Athenians. Give the masses power, and they will be so corrupted by license and egalitarianism that the first tyrant who offers to restore both will seize power by promising the people to redistribute wealth from the rich.

Starting with the first term of Thomas Jefferson in 1800, the democratic sentiments that had been held in check by the Constitution began to seek more scope. The great transformation, however, came with the Progressive movement of the late nineteenth century. The Constitution of checks and balances founded on a mistrust of human nature and its passions and interests was rejected as outmoded given the unprecedented changes wrought by science, technology, and industrialism. The power of the federal government had to increase in order to solve the numerous problems created by these changes. The Constitutional "filters" that helped limit the people from precipitately acting on their self-interests and passions, like the election of senators by state legislatures that was an important expression of federalism and state sovereignty, were weakened or eliminated. As the twentieth century progressed, under the stress of depression and war federal power expanded and created a coercive regulatory regime, an incursion upon citizen autonomy sweetened by the redistribution of property from the well off through the income tax and entitlement transfers.

Since the New Deal legislation of Franklin Delano Roosevelt and the Great Society programs of Lyndon B. Johnson, the Leviathan entitlement state has continued to expand. The republic of the founders has become more democratic, but it is a "Potemkin democracy," as James Kalb puts it, in which political freedom has become hedonistic license, while self-government and individual autonomy have been diminished by a powerful federal government, transformations made palatable by social welfare transfers.[7] This epochal change from the constitutional order of the founders in our own time has been made easier by modern developments that have perpetuated and worsened the flaws of democracy long catalogued by the antidemocratic tradition. As a result, we have created the "softer despotism" prophesized by Alexis de Tocqueville as the great danger of modern democracy.[8]

---

7. James Kalb, *The Tyranny of Liberalism* (Wilmington, DE, 2008), 46.
8. *Democracy in America*, ed. Philip Bradley, rev. Frances Bowen (New York, 1994), vol. 2, 316.

Many of democracy's flaws, from ancient Athens to the modern United States, can be traced to the perennial weaknesses and flaws of human nature that freedom and popular rule unleash. An uncritical view of democracy, then, is a kind of utopianism that ignores the tragic nature of human beings, their propensity to be driven by passions and interests rather than reason and the good. As such it can lead to policies doomed to failure because that destructive capacity of human nature is ignored or idealized. The critics of democracy from Athens to the US founding all started with a tragic view of human nature and its self-destructive passions, selfish interests, and propensity to let both override reason and fact.

Yet as the US government has evolved away from its Republican origins into something closer to Athenian democracy, the dangers and flaws of democracy acknowledged by critics for twenty-five hundred years have become more evident. Nor does it help, as classicist Loren Samons writes, that many people within the US population are confused about the type of government under which they live, a representative republic designed to protect freedom against the excesses of popular rule as well as elite dominance. In contrast, today "we believe we live in a democracy [and] we also have come to act, and to expect our political leaders and system to act, as if our government *is* a democracy (traditionally defined) and as if the popular will represents a moral 'good' in society."[9] And as the government has indeed evolved and institutionalized some of the flaws of direct democracy first analyzed in the history of ancient Athens, this confusion undermines the founders' architecture of mixed government, federalism, and the balance of power that in part was designed to check the excesses of popular government inevitably given the passions and interests of human nature.

An uncritical promotion of democracy, then, as a self-evident good beyond argument or cavil reflects the modern belief in a universal, rational human nature continually progressing beyond the destructive behaviors and passions that have marred human history and that trouble the world today. History offers little evidence that such improve-

---

9. *What's Wrong with Democracy?* (Berkeley and Los Angeles, 2004), 5.

ment has indeed taken place, or that the suspicion of either a minority or a majority monopolizing power that underlay the crafting of the Constitution is no longer necessary. The aim of this book is to recover that forgotten antidemocratic tradition and its tragic vision of human nature, and to show that the dangers and discontents of democracy still afflict us today—not, as Tocqueville wrote, "to render it weak and indolent, but solely to prevent it from abusing its aptitude and strength."[10]

---

10. *Democracy in America*, vol. 2, 323.

CHAPTER ONE

The Monitory Failures
of Athenian Democracy

The town I come from is controlled
By one man, not a mob. And there is no one
To puff it up with words, for private gain,
Swaying it this way, that way. Such a man
First flatters it with wealth of favors; then
He does it harm, but covers up his blunders
By blaming other men, and goes scot-free.
The people is no right judge of arguments;
Then how can it give right guidance to a city?
A poor man, working hard, could not attend
To public matters, even if ignorance
Were not his birthright. When a wretch, a nothing,
Obtains respect and power from the people
By talk, his betters sicken at the sight.

—Euripides, *The Suppliant Women*[1]

Around the eighth century BC the Greeks invented the idea of constitutional government.[2] Rather than rule by force that elites monopolized, the governments of the ancient polis or city-state dispersed the
power to rule throughout the whole community of free citizen males,
who collectively governed not by coercion and force controlled by men
and imposed on subjects, but by laws, institutions, offices, public deliberation, and political protocols determining the scope and limits of a

---

1. Euripides, *The Suppliant Women* 410–25, trans. Frank William Jones, in *Euripides IV* (Chicago, 1968).
2. Subsequent dates are all BC unless specified otherwise.

power now belonging to the citizenry. This citizen community was the ultimate arbiter of the state's actions, and recognized no earthly power or authority above popular sovereignty. The autonomy of the citizens in turn made them free. The Athenian orator Lysias around 400 idealized these innovative elements of constitutional government in a funeral oration. The founders of democracy, Lysias says, believed "the liberty of all to be the strongest bond of agreement; by sharing with each other the hopes born of their perils they had freedom of soul in their civic life, and used law for honoring the good and punishing the evil. For they deemed that it was the way of wild beasts to be held subject to one another by force, but the duty of men to delimit justice by law, to convince by reason, and to serve these two in act by submitting to the sovereignty of law and the instruction of reason."[3]

Not every free male, of course, could be a citizen. In the some thousand city-states of ancient Greece, citizenship could be limited to the few or expanded to the many. Some city-states were ruled by oligarchies of various stripes, with citizenship frequently defined by property qualifications or by birth. Others broadened the base of citizenship, and these were called "democracy," rule by the "many" or more accurately the *demos*, "masses." By the mid-fifth century in Athens, the "many" comprised about one-sixth of the whole population, the thirty to forty thousand adult males, whether rich or poor, noble or commoner, proven to be born of a free Athenian mother and father. This was what Aristotle called "extreme democracy," in which birth to Athenian parents was the only requirement for citizenship, and the more numerous poor dominate. As Aristotle writes, "Where the poor rule, that is a democracy." This empowerment of the poor was an "astonishing novelty," as historian Moses Finley observed, unprecedented for that time.[4]

---

3. Lysias 2.18–19, trans. W. R. M. Lamb, in *Lysias* (Cambridge, MA, and London, 1930).
4. "Extreme democracy," *Politics* 1277b and passim; trans. Benjamin Jowett, in *The Complete Works of Aristotle*, vol. 2, ed. Jonathan Barnes (Princeton, NJ, 1984); Finley in *Democracy Ancient and Modern*, rev. ed. (New Brunswick, NJ, 1985), 11; Aristotle at *Politics* 1280a, also 1317b.

More important, these citizens, whatever their class or birth, did not just have the right to vote, but they directly managed the state, being eligible with some few exceptions to serve in every public office and board that ran the city, and personally to participate in all political and judicial institutions and public deliberations that determined policy and held politicians accountable. As Pericles says of Athens in his Funeral Oration delivered at the beginning of the Peloponnesian War in 431, "Advancement in public life falls to reputation for capacity, class considerations not being allowed to interfere with merit; nor again does poverty bar the way, if a man is able to serve the state, he is not hindered by the obscurity of his condition."[5] Such a government was literally rule "of the people, by the people, and for the people."

The main organs of Athenian direct rule were the Assembly, the Council of 500, the law courts, and the numerous offices and boards responsible for the day-to-day functioning of the city and for executing both domestic and foreign policy. The Assembly was the gathering of several thousand citizens that met about forty times a year. There each citizen in attendance had the right to speak, make motions, and vote on all the policies of the state whether major or minor, domestic or foreign. The agenda for the Assembly meeting was prepared by the Council, five hundred citizens, fifty men from each of the ten Athenian "tribes" chosen by lot to serve for the whole year. For one of the ten months in the Athenian calendar each tribal contingent, the "prytany," prepared the motions or open questions to be put before the Assembly. The law courts also were in the control of ordinary citizens, rather than professional judges or prosecutors. Each year six thousand citizens were enrolled by lot in the jury pool, which provided the several hundred randomly chosen jurymen to hear a particular case, determine which laws applied, and vote on guilt or innocence. These cases resulted from indictments brought by citizens, and included, with a few exceptions, not just criminal and civil complaints but political charges as well. Finally, nearly seven hundred magistrates, the majority chosen by lot

---

5. Thucydides 2.37, trans. Richard Crawley, *The Landmark Thucydides* (New York, 1996).

and most serving a one-year term, managed the daily running of the state in matters including war, diplomacy, finance, public works and buildings, religious festivals, and theatrical presentations. At the end of their terms, they would be subjected to an "accounting" that could lead to indictment and trial, with punishments including fines or loss of citizen rights. By the early fourth century, Athenian citizens were paid to attend the Assembly, serve as a juror, and fill some offices.

Even from this brief sketch we can see how different Athenian democracy was from our own republican government, in which elected representatives debate and set policy that is implemented and managed by federal, state, and local government agencies. In addition, in Athens there was no notion of "inalienable rights" all people possessed, as rights were given by the state only to citizens, and political rights could be taken away for certain dishonorable behaviors. Yet it is the fundamental assumptions behind democratic direct rule, as well as the mechanics of governing, that critics found wrong-headed and dangerous in ways still relevant for the United States of today.

Who Is Qualified to Rule?

The notion that any man born to an Athenian mother and father was qualified to run the state was hotly disputed in antiquity. Aristocrats or *eupatridai*, those "born of good fathers," found such a notion sheer folly. To them, only noblemen belonging to ancient families that traced their ancestry to the gods possessed what the fifth-century celebrator of aristocratic athletic prowess, Pindar, called the "splendor running in the blood," a capacity for excellence, virtue, and wisdom that made them natural rulers: "The wise man knows many things in his blood," Pindar sings, "the vulgar are taught."[6]

Given the lack of innate wisdom among the *demos*, critics argued, political power in their hands could lead only to violence and disorder, particularly class warfare against the rich. A particularly gruesome

---

6. *Nemea* 3.40; *Olympia* 2.86–87; trans. Richmond Lattimore, *The Odes of Pindar* (Chicago, 1947).

example took place in the city of Miletus, a wealthy state on the coast of modern-day Turkey. There the poor seized power after a civil war and burned to death wealthy families. After the rich returned to power, they returned the favor and trampled to death with oxen many of the poor.[7] The excesses that had occurred in Megara, a city-state near Corinth, influenced the antidemocratic verses of the sixth-century poet Theognis. Plutarch described the violence of popular rule that occurred in Megara after a tyrant had been overthrown some years before Theognis was born, particularly attacks against the rich and their property. Mobs of the poor entered the homes of the rich and demanded entertainment and banquets, and if denied "they would treat all the household with violence and insult." The poor finally passed a decree allowing them to get back the interest they had paid on their debts.[8] Aristotle writes of Megara that the "demagogues drove out many of the notables in order that they might be able to confiscate their property."[9] For the aristocrat Theognis, such vicious behavior was to be expected from people "who formerly knew neither judgments or laws but clothed themselves in goatskins and wore them til they were rags and pastured themselves outside the city like deer."[10]

These prejudices against the poor masses—that they were incapable of political wisdom and virtue and perforce had base characters, and so if given power would use it to attack the well off and redistribute their property—persist throughout the antidemocratic tradition. The lack of wisdom and virtue could reflect low birth, as Pindar and Theognis suggest. But sometimes poverty itself accounts for the lack of intellectual and moral development that makes the poor unfit to rule. The earliest critic of Athenian democracy is an anonymous author conventionally called the Old Oligarch, who wrote his brief work in the second half of the fifth century. The Old Oligarch does assume the moral and intellectual superiority of the aristocracy, but then writes, "Among the

---

7. Athenaeus, *Deipnosophistae* 12.26.
8. Plutarch, *Quaestiones Graecae*, 18. In Donald Kagan, *The Great Dialogue* (New York, 1965), 36.
9. *Politics* 1304b, trans. Jowett.
10. Theognis 53–58, in Kagan, 39.

common people are the greatest ignorance, ill-discipline, and depravity. For poverty tends to lead them into base behaviour, as do lack of
education and lack of learning because of lack of money."[11] The Old
Oligarch does not address the question whether or not the poor could
be elevated from their inferiority by education or affluence. But he
consistently characterizes the ruling democratic masses in negative
terms such as "bad men," "poor men," "the worse men," the "mob," and
the "worst elements."[12]

Since the masses are badly educated and poor, they have to earn
their living by manual labor, the daily drudgery that also promotes a
lack of character and self-control. Aristotle denigrates "extreme democracy" because the citizen masses have to work, a necessity that makes
their lives "inferior" to those of farmers or herdsmen, for "there is no
room for excellence in any of their employments, whether they be arti-
sans or traders or labourers." Thus "the best form of state will not admit
them [artisans] to citizenship," for "no man can practice excellence who
is living the life of a mechanic or labourer."[13] Implicit in these remarks,
apart from obvious elitist prejudice, is the notion that governing requires
knowledge and virtue, both of which are difficult to acquire when one's
time is spent in physical labor rather than in developing the mind.

Such characterizations of the non-noble masses quickly became a
cliché in the antidemocratic tradition. Herodotus in his *Histories* (c. 430)
imagines a debate among the Persian king Darius and two courtiers
concerning the best form of government. Megabyzus, the champion of
oligarchy, scorns the "mob" as "ineffective," and says there is "nothing
more stupid or more given to brutality" than the common people. The
masses are "unruly," for "knowledge and the masses are incompatible.
How could anyone know what is right without either having been taught
or having innate awareness of it?" As such, the "general populace" is like
"a river swollen with winter rains: they rush blindly forward and sweep

---

11. *The Constitution of the Athenians* 1.5, trans. Robin Osborne, 2nd ed. (Kingston
    upon Thames, 2004).
12. At 1.1, 1.2, 1.4, 2.10, 3.10.
13. *Politics*, 1319a, 1278a, trans. Jowett.

things before them."[14] The ignorance of the volatile masses is likewise a constant theme in Thucydides's *History of the Peloponnesian War* (c. 390). In his description of his historical method, Thucydides contrasts his own painstaking effort to verify facts, with the habits of the common people, whose usual practice "is to receive [the traditions of their own country] all alike as they are delivered, without applying any critical test whatsoever," and who take little pains in investigating the truth, "accepting readily the first story that comes to hand." He explicitly links the disaster of the Sicilian Expedition of 415—in which the Athenians lost over six thousand soldiers and two hundred ships, making it exhibit number one in the traditional indictment of Athenian democracy and its excesses—to the fact that the Athenian masses were "ignorant of its size and of the number of its inhabitants, Hellenic and barbarian, and of the fact that they were undertaking a war not much inferior to that against the Peloponnesians."[15] And like Megabyzus, Thucydides comments frequently on the fickleness of the masses, swaying this way and that and changing their minds with the whim of the moment, "according to the way of the multitude," "as the multitude is wont to do," or "as is the way of a democracy," as Thucydides puts it.[16]

These critics posit a nexus between the lack of knowledge and virtue, particularly self-control over the passions and appetites, and the failures of democracy. This link is a major theme of Plato's *Apology*, a reconstruction of Socrates's defense speech at his trial in 399 for atheism and corrupting the young. At least in Plato's version, Socrates used his right to address his accusers not to get himself acquitted, but to highlight how foolish and unjust were the assumptions that any Athenian citizen had enough knowledge, virtue, and understanding to justly bring an indictment against a fellow citizen; and that several hundred randomly selected jurors could then deliberate on and decide the truth of a capital charge. According to his follower Xenophon, Socrates in contrast believed that the citizen masses comprised "dunces and weaklings,"

---

14. At 3.81, trans. Robin Waterfield (Oxford and New York, 1998).
15. 1.20, 2.1, 6.1, trans. Crawley.
16. Thucydides 2.65, 4.28, 8.1, trans. Crawley.

the "fullers or the cobblers or the builders or the smiths or the farmers or the merchants or the traffickers in the market-place who think of nothing but buying cheap and selling dear."[17] Concerned with their self-ish interests and private gain, how could they possibly have developed the disinterested knowledge or the virtue necessary to sit in judgment on questions such as what makes a good and virtuous citizen, what is the purpose of a political community, or what actions were in the long-term interest of the state?

Rather than such knowledge, Socrates argues, most people possess mere opinion, hearsay picked up from their parents or teachers or the theater, the received wisdom that they never question or examine but unthinkingly repeat as truth. And if they base political decisions and actions on this presumed truth, they are more likely to harm the state and citizens than to benefit them. Socrates makes this point by using an analogy from crafts and other specialized skills. During his defense, he recalls a conversation with an Athenian who had spent a fortune on edu-cating his two sons. If his sons were colts or calves, Socrates had asked him, it would be easy to find someone to "make them excellent in the kind of excellence proper to them; and he would be a horse-trainer or a husbandman; but now, since they are two human beings, whom have you in mind to get as a overseer? Who had knowledge of that kind of excellence, that of a man and a citizen?"

The implication, which he draws out later during his cross-examination of one of his accusers, is that "he who is able to make them [horses] better is some one person, or very few, the horse-trainers, where most people, if they have to do with and use horses, injure them," a truth that holds for people as well.[18] Neither Socrates's accusers nor the jurymen sitting in judgment have reliable knowledge of what improves the young, and so are disqualified from indicting Socrates for corrupting them, or deciding his guilt or innocence. But they arro-

---

17. At *Memorabilia* 3.7, trans. E. C. Marchant (Cambridge, MA, and London, 1923).

18. *Apology* 20b, 25b, in *Plato I. Euthyphro, Apology, Crito, Phaedo, Phaedrus*, trans. Harold North Fowler (Cambridge, MA, and London, 1914).

gantly believe they do have such knowledge because they happen to have more mundane skills. Socrates earlier had discovered the origins of this mistaken confidence during his critical "examination" of his fellow citizens about virtue and the good, the knowledge necessary for justly managing the state. Each of Socrates's interlocutors did have a particular skill, but "because of practicing his art well, each one thought he was very wise in the other more important matters, and this folly of theirs obscured that wisdom."[19] Having this ignorance publicly pointed out to them created the enmity and prejudice that has led to Socrates's indictment and ultimately his conviction and death—illustrating his point that the people make judgments based on irrational emotions like resentment or envy rather than knowledge of justice and virtue.

Socrates's most famous follower, Plato, agreed that the ignorant many could not justly and efficiently manage the state, for political wisdom and virtue were specialized skills possessed only by the few. As historian Donald Kagan writes, "the only proper basis for government is *epistêmê*, science, a body of true, unchanging wisdom open only to a few philosophers whose excellence of character and mind and devotion to philosophy have led them to a vision of reality. The training of such men requires a degree of specialization which is the very opposite of the democratic ideal of versatility."[20] Like Socrates, Plato found it ridiculous that the people would consult a ship-builder when the issue under discussion was ships, or builders when buildings were the issue, "But when the question is an affair of state, then everybody is free to have a say—tinker, cobbler, sailor, passenger; rich and poor, high and low—any one who likes gets up, and no one reproaches him" for his lack of knowledge and training.[21] Rather than rule by the many, or by the uneducated one or few, Plato in the *Republic* famously imagined a utopia in which an elite of highly trained philosophers runs a state in every way the opposite of Athens, not the least in its jettisoning of the political freedom and

---

19. *Apology* 22d–e, trans. Fowler.
20. In *The Great Dialogue*, 161.
21. *Protagoras* 319b–d, trans. Benjamin Jowett, in *The Dialogues of Plato*, vol. 1 (New York, 1937).

equal citizen rights under law that were Athens's most important contribution to Western politics.

Socrates's and Plato's skepticism that the average Athenian could have the knowledge and virtues necessary for running the state perforce indicted the Athenian practice of filling important offices by "sortition," that is, drawing lots, one of Aristotle's key components of direct democracy.[22] The use of the lot in part reflected a religious belief that the correct choice would be in the hands of the gods. But it also logically followed the assumption that every Athenian, unless disqualified by dishonorable behavior such as running away in battle or neglecting his parents, was capable of filling the office. Socrates scorned this notion, deriding "the folly of appointing public officials by lot when none would choose a pilot or a builder or a flautist by lot, nor any other craftsman for work in which mistakes are far less disastrous than mistakes in statecraft."[23] Once again, to the democracy's critics, specialized knowledge possessed only by an elite trained in wisdom and virtue is necessary for governing a state.

This belief that political wisdom is the purview of a few strikes at the heart of Athenian democracy, which believed so strongly in the capabilities of random citizens that they could be chosen to fill offices by a lottery—though military leaders were chosen by vote, a tacit admission, as some critics pointed out, that when it came to truly important offices, even the Athenians believed some people were more capable than others. To democracy's critics, sortition was foolish, since the citizen masses make life-and-death decisions based not on a knowledge that they are incapable of acquiring, but on unexamined opinions and irrational emotions. Thus as Socrates rhetorically asks his follower Crito, "In questions of right and wrong and disgraceful and noble and good and bad . . . ought we to follow and fear the opinion of the many or that of the one, if there is anyone who knows about them?"[24] Democracy's false assumption that the many indeed have such knowledge

---

22. *Rhetoric* 1365b.
23. In *Memorabilia* 1.2.9, trans. Marchant.
24. *Crito* 47d, trans. Fowler.

dooms it as a political system. From this mistake follows the other malign consequences of direct popular rule.

Ignorance Begets Demagoguery

If the masses lack the knowledge and virtue necessary to govern justly, but instead are moved by irrational passions and self-interest, then they are easy prey for political leaders who can manipulate or pander to the people in order to further their own ambitions. Such a government can succeed only if good leaders arise who can lead the masses into making the right decisions and can rein in their passionate self-interest. The great Athenian statesman Solon, whose constitutional reforms laid the foundations of the democracy around 600, set the pattern for such leaders. In a fragment from his poetry, Solon wrote, "I gave the people as much privilege as they have a right to: / I neither degraded them from rank nor gave them a free hand; / and for those who already held the power and were envied for money, / I worked it out that they should have no cause for complaint."[25] The masses were freed from oppression and given a stake in the government, but not the sort of expansive power that would allow them to redistribute the property of the rich to gratify their envy. This is the idealized early Athenian democracy that later critics continually hearken back to when attacking the radical democracy of the later fifth century.

Thucydides saw in Pericles, who guided Athens to its "golden age" starting in the mid-fifth century, a leader like Solon, one whose "rank, ability, and known integrity" allowed him "to exercise an independent control over the multitude—in short, to lead them instead of being led by them; for as he never sought power by improper means, he was never compelled to flatter them, but, on the contrary, enjoyed so high an estimation that he could afford to anger them by contradiction."[26] But the state cannot rely on such men always appearing when needed,

---

25. Fragment 5 Diehl; trans. Richmond Lattimore, *Greek Lyrics*, 2nd ed. (Chicago and London, 1960).
26. *The Peloponnesian War* 2.65, trans. Crawley.

and in a democracy, even Pericles had to be elected and reelected to the office of *strategos*, one member of the board of ten citizens that oversaw military affairs, in order to wield his influence. And a year before his death from the plague in 429, Pericles was recalled and deposed from his post as a *strategos* and fined by the people because he failed to capture Epidaurus. The lesson is that in a democracy, even a uniquely great leader is still accountable to the passions and interests of the masses.

The leaders of Athens after Pericles, in Thucydides's estimation, were much different. "More on a level with one another, and each grasping at supremacy, they ended by committing even the conduct of state affairs to the whims of the multitude." They allowed "private ambitions and private interests, in matters quite foreign to the war [against Sparta], to lead them into projects unjust both to themselves and to their allies—projects whose success would only conduce to the honor and advantage of private persons, and whose failure entailed certain disaster on the country in the war." This pandering ambition led to "blunders" like the Sicilian Expedition, which failed because the people and the politicians chose "to occupy themselves with private squabbles for the leadership of The People, by which they not only paralyzed operations in the field, but also first introduced civil discord at home."[27]

Thucydides's encomium to Pericles and his contrast with the demagogues who followed him establishes the standard by which later Athenian politicians like the ambitious, charismatic Alcibiades, the driving force behind the decision to invade Sicily, are measured. Rather than the "shepherd of the people" concerned with their long-term welfare, such leaders become "worthless demagogues," as Aristotle calls them, panderers to the people, buying their support by redistributing public money to them.[28] As Demosthenes, the last great leader of the Athenian democracy, said in 349, this "new breed of orators" asks the people, " 'What would you like? What shall I propose? How can I oblige you?' "

---

27. *The Peloponnesian War* 2.65, trans. Crawley.
28. *Politics* 1274a.

and as a consequence "the interests of the state have been frittered away for a momentary popularity."[29]

The Athenian demagogue whom Thucydides contrasts most sharply with Pericles is Cleon, for nearly a decade the most powerful politician in Athens until his death in 422 at the battle of Amphipolis. He was, according to Thucydides, "the most violent man at Athens, and at that time [427] by far the most powerful with The People."[30] Plutarch makes Cleon a class-warrior: he was "rough and heavy against the upper classes and subjected himself to the masses in order to win their favor."[31] The author of the fourth-century *Constitution of Athens*, doubtfully attributed to Aristotle, links Cleon's popularity to a new style of blustering oratory: Cleon "seems, more than any one else, to have been the cause of the corruption of the democracy by his wild undertakings; and he was the first to use unseemly shouting and coarse abuse on the Bema [the speaker's platform in the Assembly]."[32] Cleon doubled the tribute on the Athenian subject states, raised taxes on the rich, and prosecuted politicians, some say to obtain the funds necessary for buying political support—he raised the pay for jurors by a third—and perhaps enriching himself.

Cleon's most brutal critic was the comic playwright Aristophanes, who saw in Cleon the besetting flaw of democracy: it created political leaders who pandered to the people in order to further their own ambitions no matter the cost to the interests of the state or the well-being of the citizens. In Aristophanes's play the *Knights*, produced in 424, the word *demagogos* appears for the first time in surviving Greek literature, and it is used to describe Cleon. In the play, he is depicted as Paphlagon, a slave of "Demos," the personified Athenian citizenry. The slave is always "crouched" in front of Demos and "flattering and fawning and toadying

---

29. Demosthenes 3.22, trans. J. H. Vince, in *Demosthenes. Orations*, vol. I (Cambridge, MA, and London, 1930).

30. 3.36, trans. Crawley.

31. *Moralia* 807a, in Martin Ostwald, *From Popular Sovereignty to the Sovereignty of Law* (Berkeley and Los Angeles, 1986), 216.

32. AP 28, trans. F. G. Kenyon. In *The Complete Works of Aristotle*, vol. 2, ed. Jonathon Barnes (Princeton, NJ, 1984). See too Plutarch, *Life of Nicias* 8.3.

and swindling" the "cranky, half-deaf old codger," profiting from the war with Sparta and raising taxes on the rich or prosecuting them to buy the support of the poor citizens and enrich himself: "you devour public funds before you're allotted an office," the Chorus Leader scolds him.

As bad as Paphlagon/Cleon is, however, in the play he vies for the affections of Demos with a Sausage-Seller, an occupation even more base than being a tanner, as the historical Cleon was. The Sausage-Seller has all the qualities that Aristophanes, like the Old Oligarch, believes a successful democratic leader must have: he is a scoundrel from a low-born family, "ignorant and loathsome," and, like making sausages, is able to "stir up the business [of the polis], mince it all together, / And always get the people on your side" with deceiving rhetoric and bribes. Nor do the Athenian citizens come off any better. The Chorus scolds Demos, "You're easily led astray; / you enjoy being flattered / and thoroughly deceived, / and every speechmaker / has you gaping."[33] In Aristophanes's critique, the self-interested, uninformed, gullible citizenry will surrender itself to unscrupulous demagogues who promise to use state power to enrich them.

The Problem of Rhetoric in Democratic Deliberation

Woven through these critiques of democratic demagogues is the distrust of rhetoric and public oratory as an instrument of deception and manipulation. One of the great glories of constitutional government is the use of free verbal deliberation and persuasion rather than force to manage society and the state. Deliberative public speech was thus the life-blood of the democracy, the "indispensable preliminary to any wise action at all," as Pericles says in his funeral oration.[34] In Athens almost all the functions of the state took place through public speeches that tried to persuade fellow citizens to vote for one course of action rather than another. As a consequence, rhetoric, Aristotle's "art of persuasion,"

---

33. *Knights* 47–48, 42–43, 258, 115–19.
34. Thucydides 2.40, trans. Crawley.

became an important technical skill necessary for those in Athens ambitious for a political career.

Yet a skill at effective speaking could obscure the issue of right or wrong or good and bad by appealing to emotion and selfish interests rather than to principle, sound argument, and the larger good. With political power widely distributed to the citizens, the inability of the ordinary man to set aside emotion and self-interest and think critically about the good of the whole state both for now and the future made oratorical prowess a dangerous weapon in the hands of ambitious and unscrupulous leaders. In the *Republic* Plato describes the manipulation and corruption of citizens who have been aroused by a powerful orator. At any meeting of citizens, Plato writes, "there is a great uproar, and they praise some things which are being said or done, and blame other things, equally exaggerating both, shouting and clapping their hands . . . at such a time will not a young man's heart, as they say, leap within him? Will any private training enable him to stand firm against the overwhelming flood of popular opinion? Or will he be carried away by the stream? Will he not have the notions of good and evil which the public in general have—he will do as they do, and as they are, such will he be?"[35]

The ability to speak persuasively and impassion an audience allowed an orator to "make the weaker argument appear the stronger," as Socrates says—to make lies and injustice and the wrong sound like truth and justice and the right.[36] Dramatizing this point, Aristophanes in the *Clouds* (423) brings on stage a personified *Hêttôn Logos*, the "worse argument," who brags that he "pioneered the idea of arguing what's contrary to established principles of justice," and shows him out-debating and ultimately corrupting *Kreittôn Logos*, the "better argument."[37] In a direct democracy dependent for its functioning on public oratory, this skill at clever speaking conferred a power greater than wealth or physical force

35. *Republic* 492b–c, trans. Jowett.
36. *Apology* 18c, trans. Fowler.
37. *Clouds* 1038–40, trans. Jeffrey Henderson in *Aristophanes II* (Cambridge, MA, and London, 1998).

when it came to controlling the uneducated masses that sat in the
Assembly.

Plato has the rhetorician and philosopher Gorgias claim that the
greatest good, which gives men personal freedom and power over
others, is "the word which persuades the judges in the courts, or the
senators in the Council, or the citizens in the Assembly, or at any other
political meeting," and "if you have the power of uttering this word,
you will have the physician as your slave, and the trainer your slave,
and the money-maker of whom you talk will be found to gather trea-
sures, not for himself, but for you who are able to speak and persuade the
multitude." A bit later Socrates draws out the implication of Gorgias's
praise of rhetoric as a means for acquiring power apart from truth or
goodness: "The rhetorician need not know the truth about things; he
has only to discover some way of persuading the ignorant that he has
more knowledge than those who know." He does not need to know
anything about medicine, for example, to persuade the "multitude"
that he knows more than a physician. So too the orator may be "as
ignorant of the just and unjust, base and honourable, good and evil, as
he is of medicine," but all he needs is "a way with the ignorant of persuading them that he not knowing is to be esteemed to know more
about these things than some one else who knows."[38] Perceptions created by clever speaking will be more powerful than knowledge of facts
and reality.

Thucydides in his history illustrates the truth of Socrates's later
description of an amoral rhetoric as a mechanism of political power.
Repeatedly he shows us the Athenian Assembly manipulated by orators
who appeal to self-interest or some passion or other. The historian's
Mytilenean Debate stands as one of the most perceptive and influential
analyses of the malign consequences that follow when politicians skilled
at deceptive rhetoric manipulate the passions and prejudices of the
fickle, ill-informed masses. In a wonderful touch of irony, Thucydides
puts this analysis in the mouth of Cleon, the very demagogue whose
rise to power depended precisely on an oratorical style that used emo-

---

38. *Gorgias* 452e, 459a–b, trans. Jowett.

tional bluster and verbal violence rather than reasoned argument and coherent principle.

In the fifth year of the war with Sparta, a pro-Spartan faction in the city Mytilene on the island of Lesbos, a subject state of Athens, stirred up a revolt against the Athenian Empire. After the revolt was suppressed, the Athenian Assembly "in the fury of the moment" voted to kill the whole adult male population of the city and enslave the women and children. The next day, the mood of the citizens changed and the question was reopened. Cleon, who had carried the motion for the draconian punishment as an act of vengeance that would deter other cities from revolting, chastised the Assembly for its fickleness and indulgence of sentiment that he attributes to their manipulation by duplicitous orators.

These clever men, Cleon thunders, "are always wanting to appear wiser than the laws, and to overrule every proposition brought forward, thinking that they cannot show their wit in more important matters, and by such behavior too often ruin their country" by indulging "cleverness and intellectual rivalry." But Cleon blames the citizens as well as the clever orators: "The persons to blame are you who are so foolish as to institute these contests; who go to see an oration as you would to see a sight, take your facts on hearsay, judge of the practicability of a project by the wit of its advocates, and trust for the truth as to past events, not to the fact which you saw more than to the clever strictures which you heard; the easy victims of new-fangled arguments, unwilling to follow received conclusions; slaves to every new paradox, despisers of the commonplace," and in a striking phrase, "very slaves to the pleasure of the ear, and more like the audience of a rhetorician than the Council of a city."[39]

No passage in Greek literature better sets out the dangers that arise when the masses are empowered to deliberate and decide the most important state policies through the medium of a public oratory vulnerable to the artful manipulations of the speaker. Cleon saves his harshest criticism for the people, who do not use rational analysis or critical

---

39. Thucydides 3.37–38, trans. Crawley.

thinking to judge proposals, but rather see the speeches as a form of entertainment and base their vote on the pleasure a speaker arouses rather than on the soundness and coherence of his argument. Implicit in Cleon's analysis is the assumption that the people do not have the mental acuity or training to privilege the "fact which you saw" over the "clever strictures" of the speakers "who charm us with sentiment," leaving the city to pay a "heavy penalty" for the "momentary pleasure" received from such speeches.[40]

Despite being a populist demagogue, Cleon has indicted the Athenian Assembly in terms redolent of the antidemocratic, elitist critiques of the Old Oligarch or Socrates. Both Cleon's angry appeal to vengeance against the Mytileneans, which exploited the anger of the Athenians, and his political career itself confirm the charge against democracy made by the Old Oligarch: that the democracy serves its own interests "in allowing even the bad to speak. For if the good spoke and served on the Council, there would be excellent consequences for those like them, but not excellent consequences for those sympathetic with the common people." The citizens in the Assembly "recognize that this man's [the bad speaker's] ignorance and depravity and goodwill profit them more than the good man's ability, wisdom, and ill-will."[41] In a democracy, the citizens' self-interest trumps the bad character of the politician, as long as he delivers the goods. A vicious feedback loop is created between the ambitions of the politicians and the selfish interests of the people.

In the event, the Athenians voted, just barely, to rescind the slaughter of the innocent along with the guilty, convinced not by pity or justice but by the cold calculation of self-interest and expediency advanced by Cleon's rival Diodotus. In Thucydides's next great example of the Assembly's manipulation by a demagogue, the debate over the Sicilian Expedition, it is the lure of benefits the citizens hoped to gain from the expedition that leads them to authorize the military disaster that followed their attack on the powerful city of Syracuse.

---

40. Thucydides 3.40, trans. Crawley.
41. *Constitution of the Athenians* 1.6–1.7, trans. Osborne.

The debate contrasts the sober arguments against the expedition made by Nicias, with the appeals to personal gain, an expanded empire, and nationalist glory advanced by the ambitious Alcibiades. After the Assembly quickly approved the expedition, another meeting was held to vote on equipping the ships and funding the generals. Nicias, who believed that "the state was not well advised, but upon a slight and specious pretext was aspiring to the conquest of the whole of Sicily," Thucydides writes, took the opportunity to try and change the Athenians' minds by laying out the dangers and difficulties of such a great enterprise.[42] He reminded the Assembly of the still serious threat from the Spartans and the shakiness of the peace treaty that had suspended hostilities, an ongoing revolt of a city to the north in Thrace, and the ill will of other subject states ripe for revolt if the Athenians should suffer a setback. He pointed out how distant Sicily was from Athens, about eight hundred miles, the power and numbers of the Syracusans, and the difficulty of ruling such a distant subject state even if the Athenians should succeed. Most importantly, he counseled prudence when Athens still had an unresolved conflict with a powerful nearby rival, Sparta, with whom the Athenians had fought a battle a few years earlier at Mantinea. He correctly advises that the Athenians' "struggle, therefore, if we are wise, will not be for the barbarian Egestaeans [the city in Sicily that had asked for Athens's help] but to defend ourselves most effectively against the oligarchic machinations of Sparta." He also warns the Athenians against the ambitions of Alcibiades, who hopes to "maintain his private splendor at his country's risk" and nurses a "mad dream of conquest."[43]

Nicias's advice was rational and prudent, and based on some of the factors that in the end helped to doom the expedition. Alcibiades, in contrast, appealed to the lure of wealth and glory that would accrue to Athens from the conquest of Syracuse and the expansion of their empire. Alcibiades was "by far the warmest advocate of the expedition," according to Thucydides, for he was "exceedingly ambitious of a command by which he hoped to reduce Sicily and Carthage, and personally to gain in

---

42. Thucydides 6.11, trans. Crawley.
43. Thucydides 6.11, 6.12, 6.13, trans. Crawley.

wealth and reputation by means of his success."[44] In his response to
Nicias he holds out the prospect that by conquering Sicily "we shall
either become masters, as we very easily may, of the whole of Hellas
[Greece], or in any case ruin the Syracusans, to the no small advantage
of ourselves and our allies." But he also suggests an even greater prize,
the extension of the empire beyond Greece: "We cannot fix the exact
point at which our empire shall stop; we have reached a position in
which we must not be content with retaining what we have but must
scheme to extend it, for if we cease to rule others, we shall be in danger
of being ruled ourselves." Later, after Alcibiades defects to the Spartans,
he tells them, "We sailed to Sicily first to conquer, if possible, the Sicil-
ians, and after them the Italians also, and finally to assail the empire and
city of Carthage." If Alcibiades is telling the truth about Athenian ambitions, the aim was to conquer nearly the whole Mediterranean. Since the
Athenian Empire was based on a powerful fleet rowed in the main for
pay by the Athenian poor, the prospect of expanding the empire promised more wages for rowing, and more loot and tribute from new subject
states available for transfer payments to the citizens.[45]

Nicias responded to the obvious support of the Assembly by giving
his highest estimate of the size and the costs of the expedition to deter
them by the expense. Yet this ploy backfired, as the riches dangled
before the Assembly and the grandeur of the enterprise unwittingly
enhanced by Nicias exploited both the self-interests and irrational passions of the Assembly members: "The Athenians, however, far from
having their enthusiasm for the voyage destroyed by the burdensome-
ness of the preparations, became more eager for it than ever." Indeed,
Thucydides makes explicit the intensity of the Athenians' irrational
desire for wealth and glory: "Everyone fell in love with the enterprise.
The older men thought they would either subdue the places against
which they were to sail, or at all events, with so large a force, meet
with no disaster; those in the prime of life felt a longing for foreign
sights and spectacles, and had no doubt that they should come safe

---

44. Thucydides 6.15, trans. Crawley.
45. Thucydides 6.18, 6.90, trans. Crawley.

home again; while the idea of the common people and the soldiery was to earn wages at the moment [the treasury increased the pay for seamen, and the commanders added bonuses as well], and make conquests that would supply a never-ending fund of pay for the future."[46] The translation "fell in love" does not capture the full intensity of the Greek, which says more literally, "Sexual passion [*erôs*] for the enterprise attacked all of them." Thucydides here shows us the power of the irrational working in the masses, whose decisions and policies reflect both their passions and their greed. Clever speakers are able to exploit both for their own ambitions, and both can be gratified by the political power of the masses.

Democracy and the Redistribution of Wealth

A common thread running through all the attacks on Athenian democracy is the charge that the common people and the poor, envious of the wealth of the rich, will use their political power to redistribute property.[47] This class conflict was assumed to be the natural state of things, given an irrational human nature and the unequal distribution of talent, hard work, birth, and luck among people. In Plato's *Republic* Socrates sees this conflict as endemic to every polis, which is in reality two cities, "one the city of the poor, the other of the rich; these are at war with one another."[48] Although such redistribution and cancellation of debts took place in some Greek cities, the actual redistribution of land was rare in Athens, forbidden by law. The chief civic magistrate called the Eponymous Archon at the start of his term issued a proclamation "that whatever any one possessed before he entered into office, that he shall possess and hold until the end of his term." So too the jurors, who swore, "I will not allow private debts to be cancelled, nor lands nor houses belonging to Athenian citizens to be redistributed."[49]

---

46. Thucydides 6.24, trans. Crawley.
47. See, for example, Aristotle *Politics* 1281a, 1318a; AP 40.
48. *Republic* 422e–23, trans. Benjamin Jowett, in *The Dialogues of Plato*, vol. 1 (1892; New York, 1937).
49. Demosthenes 24.149, trans. A. T. Murray, in Kagan, 84; AP 56, trans. Kenyon.

The radical democracy found indirect mechanisms for providing the masses with funds in addition to transferring wealth from the rich through various forms of taxation. The Athenian Empire itself, as Loren Samons writes, "encouraged not only the radicalization of the democracy though public payments but also the continuation of imperial policies," since the tribute collected from the empire's subject states provided funds for distribution to citizens through building programs, public shows and religious processions, allotments of conquered land given to Athenian colonists, and pay to row in the fleet on the regular missions that enforced Athens's control of its subjects. Thus, Samons continues, "the citizenry encouraged the extension or more efficient exploitation of the empire," and Athens's harsh treatment of its fellow free Greeks "was one result of the democratic Athenian citizens' determination to empower themselves and achieve greatness at the expense of other Greeks."[50] As payments from subject states diminished and then disappeared after the Peloponnesian War, various direct and indirect transfers from wealthier Athenians became another source of money for the citizens. This was a more subtle form of wealth distribution than the outright seizure of property feared by antidemocracy critics, for transfers of state money to citizens in part amounted to a transfer of wealth from the rich to the poor.

An important source of income for Athenian citizens was the pay they received for attending the Assembly, serving on a jury or on the Council, and filling some offices. Critics of democracy saw pay for service as the corrupting innovation that made the citizen's relationship to the state a mercenary rather than patriotic one, and that also corrupted politicians into buying the support of voters to further their own ambitions. Pericles instituted the first state pay, for jury service, around 450. According to the *Constitution of Athens*, he did this "as a bid for popular favour to counterbalance the wealth of Cimon," his political rival. As a result, Pericles caused "a deterioration in the character of the juries, since it was always the common people who put themselves forward for selection," and contributed to legitimizing the

---

50. *What's Wrong with Democracy*, 83. Emphases omitted.

practice of bribery.[51] This account may be historically doubtful, but it is consistent with the common view about the corrupting influence of pay for service. Plato has Socrates say of Pericles, "He was the first who gave the people pay, and made them idle and cowardly, and encouraged them in the love of talk and money."[52] In Aristophanes's *Women at Assembly*, the Chorus contrasts the corrupt present with the good old days when "none would have dared to let himself be paid for the trouble he spent over public business. . . . The citizen has become as mercenary as the stonemason."[53] These criticisms reflected the elitist prejudice that the common people always are motivated by personal gain rather than principled duty.

By the early fourth century, an Athenian citizen had other opportunities for earning state pay. In addition to jury service, citizens received compensation for attendance at the Assembly and serving in most offices. And the rowers were paid while serving in the fleet. To Aristotle, this pay for public service was, like selection of magistrates by lot, one of the fundamental institutions of the radical democracy, for it ensured the supremacy of the common people: "When they are paid, the common people have the most leisure, for they are not hindered by the care of their property, which often fetters the rich, who are thereby prevented from taking part in the assembly or in the courts, and so the state is governed by the poor, who are the majority, and not by the laws."[54] Moreover, distributing state pay only leads to more demands, for "the poor are always receiving and always wanting more and more, for such help is like water poured into a leaky cask."[55] Modern scholars question whether state pay—at barely around a day laborer's wage for one day, it was modest at best—was ample enough to make the masses "idle and lazy," or "mercenary," or in possession of the "most leisure." But the antidemocratic tradition made pay for public service one of the flaws

---

51. AP 27, trans. Kenyon.
52. *Gorgias* 515d, trans. Jowett.
53. *Women at Assembly* 304–6, 308–10. Trans. In *The Complete Greek Drama* (New York, 1938).
54. *Politics* 1313b, quote 1293a, trans. Jowett.
55. *Politics* 1320a, trans. Jowett.

in the system that corrupted the relationship of citizen to state by weakening civic virtue and duty. For democracy's critics, the Athenian government was, to borrow the topic of a Winston Churchill article, "Government of the/by the/for the dole-drawers."

In the early fourth century, Athens created the Second Athenian League, which generated more wealth for the state from tribute payments, but not nearly as much as the earlier Athenian Empire had enjoyed in the fifth century.[56] Additionally, the great wealth Athens had extracted for nearly a century from the silver mines at Laurium declined considerably. The Athenians had also amassed a large debt, some seven thousand talents, owed to the gods from whose temple treasuries they had borrowed money during the Peloponnesian War. Yet despite the reduction in revenues and the debt to the gods, another source of payment to citizens was created, the "theoric" fund (*theorikon*). This was a stipend for attendance at religious festivals, including those at which tragedy was performed. At first, any revenue surpluses were distributed annually to two funds, the military and the theoric. But in the mid-fourth century a law was passed that transferred the entire surplus to the theoric fund, and a few years later another law made it a capital crime to transfer money from the theoric to the military fund.

The amount spent on the theoric fund, about fifteen talents, was not enormous.[57] But the theoric fund was particularly insidious, for both rich and poor liked it: the former for the money, the latter because it substituted for a tax on their wealth. Hence it was, as the orator Demades, a contemporary of Demosthenes, called it, the "glue of the democracy," something that transcended social class.[58] But it was recognized in antiquity as having a corrupting effect on the citizens by fostering an entitlement mentality that made such payments a greater priority than spending on defense. In 351 Demosthenes pointed out in a speech, "While the sum of money you are discussing is a trifle, the habit of

---

56. Annual income in the mid-fifth century was about a thousand talents, compared to about four hundred in the mid-fourth century. A talent of silver was roughly equivalent to the wages of six thousand men for one day (Samons, 80).
57. A. H. M. Jones, *Athenian Democracy* (1957; Baltimore, MD, 1986), 33.
58. In Jones, 35.

mind it fosters is a serious matter."[59] Demosthenes goes on to define that "habit of mind" as the expectation of receiving public money without being willing personally to serve the state, particularly in fulfilling military obligations. Decades earlier Aristophanes had articulated the same danger arising from state pay, when the Sausage-Seller of the *Knights*, scolding Demos, says, "If two politicians were making proposals, one to build long ships [i.e., warships] and the other to spend the same on state pay, the pay man would walk all over the trireme man."[60] Sacrificing for defense generally loses out to continuing entitlement payments.

Between pay for performing civic duties and the theoric dole, by the mid-fourth century "many Athenian citizens," M. H. Hansen writes, "could expect a state payment of one kind or another, *misthos* [state pay] on working days, and *theorikon* on festival days."[61] As we shall see later, the failure of the Athenians to respond in a timely fashion to the Macedonian Philip II's two decades of expansionary aggression was partly a consequence of the decline of personal civic responsibility among Athenians who preferred to serve their own private interests rather than those of the state. Theopompus, a historian contemporary with Philip's conquest of Athens in 338, wrote that the Athenian Eubulus, who had convinced the Athenians to transfer all surplus revenue into the theoric fund and managed it for several years, made the Athenians "less courageous and more lax" by giving them the theoric dole, upon which "the Athenian people thoroughly squandered their state revenues," spending "more on public festivals and sacrifices than on the management of the war."[62]

Theopompus perhaps exaggerates the amount of money spent on the fund, but he accurately makes the connection between the decline in the citizens' willingness to make sacrifices for the well-being of the state,

59. Demosthenes 13.2, trans. Vince.
60. *Knights* 1350–53, trans. Henderson.
61. In *The Athenian Democracy in the Age of Demosthenes* (Berkeley and Los Angeles, 1991), 98.
62. Theopompus Fragments 99, 100, 213, trans. C. B. Gulick, in Gordon S. Shrimpton, *Theopompus the Historian* (Montreal and Kingston, 1991).

and the receipt of state money doled out by politicians. Demosthenes made the same connection, in his speech of 351 trying to rouse the Athenians to meet the challenge of Philip: "The politicians hold the purse-strings and manage everything, while you, the people, robbed of nerve and sinew, stripped of wealth and allies, have sunk to the level of lackeys and hangers-on, content if the politicians gratify you with a dole from the Theoric Fund or a [religious] procession."[63]

Where did the money come from for funding the state and these various transfers to citizens? There were "sundry taxes, rents of public and sacred lands, and mining royalties and concession prices," and "fees, fines and confiscations imposed by the courts."[64] Most of the wealth came from the better off. A property tax called the *eisphora* excluded the poorer citizens, with about one-third to one-fourth of the citizens subjected to this tax. Sometimes called a "war tax," it was a way for revenues to be raised for defense at the expense of property-owners. At first it was gathered only during emergencies, but by the mid-fourth century it had become an annual tax. This tax was not particularly onerous on the wealthy, and it could hit what we would call middle-class citizens as well. But it came on top of a more burdensome obligation on the wealthy, the "liturgies." These were financial and personal obligations wealthier citizens performed for the benefit of the whole citizenry. By Demosthenes's time the "trierarchy" required four hundred rich men to pay for part of the cost of maintaining a trireme, including the pay for the rowers, which could be as much as a whole talent.[65] The other major liturgy imposed on the rich an obligation to pay for one of the cult festivals in honor of the gods. This expense was considerably less than that of a trierarchy. The most famous festival liturgy was the "choregia," which required the wealthy citizen to finance the expenses of the choruses that performed in tragedies, comedies, and other productions in the some one hundred festivals a year celebrated in honor of various gods. There also was the "gymnasia," a liturgy that paid for training

---

63. Demosthenes 3.31, trans. Vince.
64. Jones, *Athenian Democracy*, 101–2.
65. Hansen, 111.

the teams that ran in the torch-races that were part of some religious festivals.

Many wealthy citizens were eager to undertake the expense of a liturgy for the status it gave them as a benefactor of the masses, something particularly useful if a rich man found himself in a trial before a jury of several hundred Athenian citizens. Additionally, class resentments that might fester into revolution could be mitigated by this public largess. Yet on top of the property tax, liturgies added to the financial burdens of a small elite of wealthy citizens who "minister to the state with their property," as Aristotle put it, financing much of the expense of running the democracy for the benefit of the masses.[66] The Old Oligarch certainly viewed liturgies as a redistribution of property from the rich to the poor: "The common people think that they deserve to take money for singing and running and dancing and sailing in the ship, so that they get more and the rich become poorer."[67]

The fourth-century orator Isocrates likewise linked the liturgies to class envy. While defending himself at a trial in which another rich man shifted his liturgical burden onto Isocrates by claiming the orator was richer than he, a legal procedure called *antidosis*, Isocrates claims, "A man has to be ready to defend himself against being rich as if it were the worst of crimes, and to keep on the alert if he is to avoid disaster; for it has become far more dangerous to be suspected of being well off than to be detected in crime; for criminals are pardoned or let off with slight penalties, while the rich are ruined utterly, and it will be found that the number of men who have been spoiled of their property is greater than those who have been punished for their misdeeds."[68] And the facilitators of this despoliation are the "depraved orators and demagogues," as Isocrates calls them in another speech, who "want to see all of our citizens reduced to the condition of helplessness in which they themselves are powerful. And the greatest proof of this is that they do not consider

---

66. *Politics* 1291a, trans. Jowett.
67. *Constitution of the Athenians* 1.13, trans. Osborne.
68. 15.160, trans. George Norlin, in *Isocrates II* (Cambridge, MA, and London, 1929).

by what means they may provide a livelihood for those who are in need, but rather how they may reduce those who are thought to possess some wealth to the level of those who are in poverty."[69] For all the exaggerations of these complaints, we see here the nexus of class envy, venal and ambitious politicians, and redistribution of wealth that runs throughout the antidemocratic tradition.

Accountability and Democracy

As important for constitutional government as the institutionalizing of power in laws and offices rather than in men was the ability of the citizens to hold those who used state power accountable for their actions. For the Athenians, the public accountability of politicians was, like the freedom to participate in public deliberation and the broad access to state offices, a foundation of their political freedom. The tragic poet Aeschylus, contrasting the quasi-divine, autocratic Persian King Xerxes with the free Athenians in his play the *Persians*, has Xerxes's mother say that even if his invasion of Greece fails, her son "is not answerable to the state; / and safe returned, he holds this land in sway even as before." The word translated "answerable" (*hupeuthunos*) is a compound of the technical term (*euthyna*) for the procedure of accountability every Athenian magistrate was subjected to after his one-year term of office was over.[70] As necessary as accountability was for limiting abuses of power and thus protecting political freedom, however, its excesses and politicized misuse made it another way the masses could control and manipulate politicians and punish them for either not serving the interests of the people, or angering them by their policies, no matter how necessary or useful for the good of the whole state. And accountability was a powerful tool for politicians to use against factional rivals.

---

69. 8.129–31, trans. Norlin.
70. *Persians* 213–14, trans. H. Weir Smith, *Aeschylus I* (Cambridge, MA, and London, 1922); cf. also Herodotus 3.80, where another compound, *aneuthynos*, "unaccountable," characterizes monarchy.

The scrutinizing pressure the city put on its leaders and citizens, moreover, was in some ways much more intense than what we experience today. Athens was a small town, and all public business was conducted face-to-face through public speaking. This civic intimacy made even private behavior more public and hence a concern of the people, who could judge it a sign of political unworthiness or danger to the state, no matter how able the citizen may have been otherwise. For example, an Athenian could lose his citizen rights by throwing away his shield in battle, neglecting his parents or their graves, squandering his inheritance, or allowing another man to use him sexually like a woman. Politicians and magistrates particularly were subject to intense scrutiny of their behavior. Any Athenian could approach a politician or magistrate in the marketplace, or at a religious festival, or at the theater, and question or criticize him, as Socrates did. This scrutiny made political leaders continually and directly subject to the judgment and criticism of their fellow citizens who disapproved of their policies or decisions. Socrates was not overly exaggerating at his trial when he told the Athenian jurors, "The fact is that no man will save his life who nobly opposes you or any other populace and prevents many unjust and illegal things from happening in the state. A man who really fights for the right, if he is to preserve his life for even a little while, must be a private citizen, not a public man."[71]

The Athenian democracy had several institutions that policed and scrutinized political behavior to make sure the politicians and magistrates served the people's interests, and that imposed punishments ranging from fines to death on those judged to have betrayed or ignored those interests. In the fifth century, "ostracism" was a formal mechanism for banishing a citizen for ten years for no reason other than that at least six thousand citizens had written his name on a fragment of pottery (*ostrakon*). The random, subjective, or impulsive nature of ostracism illustrated the irrational decision-making of citizens frequently highlighted by critics. Plutarch tells of an illiterate citizen who asked the early fifth-century politician Aristides the Just to write down Aristides's name for

---

71. *Apology* 32a, trans. Fowler.

ostracism. When Aristides asked why, the citizen replied that he was sick of hearing Aristides called the "Just." In Plutarch's analysis, ostracism was "a merciful exorcism of the spirit of jealous hate," a way that the class envy endemic to democracy could be expressed without destructive violence.[72] By the fourth century other procedures for holding politicians account-able had replaced ostracism.

Before entering office, magistrates faced an examination (*dokimasia*) that asked about their family, religious practices, political beliefs, mili-tary record, and tax payments, with witnesses required to substantiate the candidates' answers. The last step in the vote for confirmation was an open invitation for any citizen who objected to the candidate to raise his concerns.[73] During his one-year term, a magistrate was subjected to a regular "vote on the magistrates," basically a vote of no confidence proposed by any citizen. The Council regularly inspected magistrates' accounts and entertained accusations against them. These accusations could lead to trials and various punishments upon conviction.

The *euthyna* mentioned above was the formal investigation held at the end of the magistrate's term that required the office-holder or any-one carrying out public business or handling public money to account for his spending, or answer charges of embezzlement or bribery. In addition, his general behavior while in office was scrutinized. Any citi-zen could make any sort of charge against a magistrate, and if judged by the board of ten inspectors to be actionable, the magistrate would be tried in court, with a punishment ranging from a fine to death, though no evidence exists that any magistrate was ever executed. In the exami-nations held before, during, and after leaving office, the opportunity for any citizen to make a charge against the magistrate created a mech-anism for applying partisan political pressure on those running the state. This danger may lie behind the quip Plutarch attributes to Alcibiades. When told his guardian Pericles was "studying how to render his accounts to the Athenians," Alcibiades answered, "Would it not be

---

72. *Aristides* 7.2, 7.6, trans. Bernadotte Perrin, *Plutarch Lives*, vol. 2 (Cambridge, MA, and London, 1914).
73. See AP 55.

better for him to study how not to render his accounts to the Athenians?"[74] The jurors who sat in judgment of politicians indeed were to be feared, as Aristophanes, no doubt exaggerating, says in his play the *Wasps:* "From the moment I leave my bed," a juror brags, "men of power, the most illustrious in the city, await me at the bar of the tribunal; the moment I am seen from the greatest distance, they come forward to offer me a gentle hand."[75]

Another serious charge against a politician in the fourth century was the *graphe paranomon*, a citizen's allegation that a particular decree passed by the Assembly was contrary to the constitution, whether on technical or more substantive grounds, or was damaging to the interests of the people or to democratic principles. The charge was tried before a jury of at least 501 citizens. Whoever made the motion on which the Assembly voted was held personally accountable, not the citizens who may have voted for it. For example, after news of the disaster at Syracuse reached Athens, Thucydides writes, the people "were angry with the orators who had joined in promoting the expedition, just as if they had not themselves voted it."[76] A conviction typically brought a fine that could be substantial, or a loss of citizen rights. The logic behind this strange procedure arises from the problems with public speaking and manipulative rhetoric discussed above: "The philosophy behind the penalty," M. H. Hansen writes, "was . . . that the people are never wrong, and will indubitably reach the right decision if a matter is properly put to them, but they can be misled by cunning and corrupt orators and make erroneous decisions against their better judgments."[77] Such trials may have occurred on average once a month, meaning that proposals were second-guessed and proposers punished on a regular basis, not necessarily because the decree was harmful or illegal, but because the people were dissatisfied with the result, or a political enemy was using the charge to weaken a political rival.

---

74. Plutarch, *Alcibiades*, 7.2; in Kagan, *The Great Dialogue*, 88–89.
75. *Wasps* 550–54, ed. Eugene O'Neill, in *The Complete Greek Drama*, vol. 2 (New York, 1938).
76. Thucydides 8.1, trans. Crawley.
77. In *The Athenian Democracy*, 207.

Finally, the "denunciation" (*eisangelia*) was a charge brought before the Assembly against anyone suspected of overthrowing the democracy or joining a conspiracy to do so, betraying the city, fleet, or army to the enemy, or accepting a bribe to gull the Assembly into making a decision harmful to the city.[78] Anyone so accused faced the penalty of a fine or even death if convicted. And unlike other trials, the accuser faced no penalty if he got less than one-fifth of the jury's votes, making frivolous or politically motivated charges more likely. These trials, then, were obviously political, often originating in factional rivalries or conflicts. They were a potent means for the most democratic of Athenian institutions, the courts, to impose control over politicians and especially the board of ten elected "generals" who oversaw military affairs. By M. H. Hansen's calculation, a fifth of all the generals between 432 and 355 were subjected to denunciation.[79]

Frequently such charges were generated by passionate, if not irrational, responses to setbacks and failures in war. As such it was a toxic example of the otherwise critical constitutional principle of civilian control of the military. A notorious instance of the abuses such a vaguely worded law could generate came during the last years of the Peloponnesian War. After the sea-battle near Arginusae in 406, the eight victorious Athenian generals were denounced and tried en masse contrary to the law because a storm had prevented them from rescuing the shipwrecked sailors. The six who returned to Athens to stand trial were convicted and executed. The threat of such second-guessing and the lethal penalties that punished military leaders no doubt compromised their effectiveness, as Demosthenes complained when scolding Athens for its lethargy in resisting Philip: "So scandalous is our present system that every general is tried two or three times for his life in your courts, but not one of them dares to risk death in battle against the enemy."[80]

---

78. Denunciation before the council involved government officials accused of maladministration.
79. Hansen, 217.
80. Demosthenes 4.47, trans. Vince.

The critics of Athenian democracy found a more venal motive for political trials—money. Given that any citizen could charge someone with an offense, the so-called "sycophants" initiated prosecutions in order to get money either from the person charged, who feared a trial in which an experienced orator argued before several hundred random jurors, or from someone else who wanted a political enemy or rival prosecuted. Some charges upon conviction awarded the accuser one-half of the fine or three-quarters of confiscated property.[81] Sycophants were frequently lumped together with demagogic orators as the prime corrupters of the state.[82] In times of financial stress, confiscating the wealth of those found guilty in a trial could provide more funds for distribution to the people. In a defense speech from 399, Lysias begins by saying of the accusers, "You [the jury] should bear in mind the assertion that you have often heard from the mouths of these men, whenever they sought to ruin somebody unjustly—that, unless you make the convictions that they demand, your stipends will not be forthcoming."[83] Later Plato makes the same charge, saying of the people, "Do not their leaders deprive the rich of their estates and distribute them among the people; at the same time taking care to reserve the larger part for themselves?"[84] How often this actually happened can be disputed, but the charge is consistent with the basic antidemocratic belief that the fickle and greedy masses, stirred up by ambitious demagogues, will use the institutions of democratic accountability to redistribute wealth from the rich to the poor.

Finally, the high level of citizen participation in governing the democracy meant that conflicting political factions had wide scope for pursuing their partisan interests, often at the expense of the long-term interests of the state as a whole. The most obvious conflict was that

---

81. *Phasis*, the crime of smuggling goods into Athens without paying custom duties, awarded the informer one-half of the property; *apagogê*, the crimes of illegally enjoying citizen rights, or stealing, awarded three-quarters of confiscated property.
82. Cf., for example, *Isocrates* 15.314–18. The origins of the term "sycophant" for these blackmailers, literally "fig-shower," are obscure.
83. Lysias 27.1, trans. Lamb.
84. *Republic* 565a, trans. Jowett. Cr. Aristotle, *Politics* 1305a.

between rich and poor, which Plato above described as a perpetual war in every city. There was also a broad division between those who favored a more oligarchic constitution and those who supported the radical democracy. Individual politicians, ambitious for power and influence, competed with others through the institutions of the democracy, from the policies argued for and voted on in the Assembly, to the numerous political trials generated by the mechanisms of accountability described above. This incessant competition and conflict were frequently decried as a great danger to Athens. Xenophon has the son of Pericles criticize Athenian factionalism as the cause of the city's decline: Athenians lack "harmony" and "instead of working together for the general good, they are more envious and bitter against one another than against the rest of the world, are the most quarrelsome of men in public and private assemblies, most often go to law with one another, and would rather make profit of one another so than by mutual service, and while regarding public affairs as alien to themselves, yet fight over them too. . . . So it comes about that mischief and evil grow apace in the city, enmity and mutual hatred spring up among the people."[85]

The Greek word for this factionalism was *stasis*, which could mean, "party," "faction," "sedition," "discord," but also "civil war" or "revolution," indicating how destructive factional rivalries could be.[86] Thucydides has left a famous description of the horrific violence and anarchy that can rend a state when such partisanship erupts into civil war. Surveying the crimes and corruption that befell the island of Corcyra when the democratic pro-Athenian and the oligarchic pro-Spartan factions fought each other in 427 during the Peloponnesian War, Thucydides highlights the extremes of both sides, whose leaders "made the fairest professions: on the one side with a cry of political equality of The People, on the other of a modest aristocracy; but they sought prizes for themselves in those public interests which they pretended to cherish and, stopping at nothing in their struggles for ascendancy, engaged in direct excesses." Thus Corcyra became the "first example" of the worst crimes of civil war, "of

---

85. In *Memorabilia* 3.5.16–17, trans. Marchant.
86. Finley, *Democracy Ancient and Modern*, 44–45.

the reprisals exacted by the governed who had never experienced equitable treatment or indeed anything but insolence from their rulers—when their hour came; of the iniquitous resolves of those who desired to get rid of their accustomed poverty and ardently coveted their neighbor's goods; and lastly, of the savage and pitiless excesses into which men who had begun the struggle not in a class but in a party spirit, were hurried by their ungovernable passions."[87] Here the critics of democracy see the grim wages of empowering the irrational passions and selfish interests of the masses manipulated and bribed by venal and ambitious politicians.

The Flaws of Democracy and Foreign Policy

The critics of the radical Athenian democracy, historian Paul Rahe writes, have charged "that the city's legal and judicial system fostered a pattern of malicious prosecution, which made Athens unsafe for men of exceptional wealth, talent, or intelligence, and that her assembly provided a middle ground more conducive to passionate outburst than to rational deliberation, rendering Athenian politics so tumultuous, turbulent, and contentious that it was virtually impossible for a statesman to pursue a coherent foreign policy."[88] For most of Athens's history, the democracy promoted an aggressive foreign policy, contrary to the common belief today that democracies are inherently less bellicose. In the fifth century, Athens created its empire, subjecting about one hundred other free Greek states in order to generate the revenues for payments to citizens and for enhancing the glory of the city. "At Athens," Samons writes, "democracy fostered an empire, and the empire in turn made democracy practicable and profitable."[89]

During the fifth century, the flaws of radical democracy compromised foreign policy and ultimately led to Athens's defeat and near-destruction by Sparta. The Sicilian Expedition of 415 discussed above is

---

87. Thucydides 3.82, 3.84, trans. Crawley.
88. In *The Ancien Régime in Classical Greece*, 193
89. *What's Wrong with Democracy?*, 116.

the most obvious example of a military decision resulting from the passions and interests of the Assembly rather than a sound strategy. But more important was the relentless second-guessing of policy that led to the "denunciation" and subsequent trials of military leaders who angered the people, something that deterred the more talented from public service. Obviously, blaming generals for the bad policies approved by the Assembly was a way for citizens to avoid responsibility for their own bad judgment. Worse yet, such scrutiny created risk-aversion and a preference for short-term planning dangerous during a war. As Moses Finley writes, "The week-by-week conduct of a war . . . had to go before the Assembly week by week, as if Winston Churchill were to have been compelled to take a referendum before each move in World War II, and then to face another vote after the move was made, in the Assembly or the law-courts, to determine not merely what the next step should be but also whether he was to be dismissed and his plans abandoned, or even whether he was to be held criminally culpable, subject to a fine or exile, or, conceivably, given the death penalty either for the proposal itself or for the way the previous move had been carried out."[90] Pericles, the fifth-century general Demosthenes, Phormio, Nicias, Alcibiades, and Conon, to name the most famous generals of this period, were all punished by the Assembly, or withdrew from service because of the fear they would be. The historian Thucydides himself was banished for twenty years from Athens after the loss of Amphipolis to the Spartans in 422, where he was sent as one of the generals.

A few decades after Athens's defeat at the hands of Sparta and its loss of the empire, it formed the Second Athenian League to increase funds for redistribution through state pay, and to recover its prestige as a major power. By the mid-fourth century, however, the Athenians increasingly became unwilling to sacrifice both their own time and revenues in order to protect their interests, now threatened by Philip II of Macedon. In the view of leaders like Demosthenes, the flaws of democracy outlined above contributed to Athens's ultimate defeat and loss of its political freedom at the battle of Chaeronea in 338.

---

90. In *Democracy Ancient and Modern*, 59–60.

The denunciations and trials of generals illustrate an endemic weakness of constitutional governments that give political power to large numbers of citizens—the public deliberation and procedures of governing can become dangerous during times of crises, particularly when the enemy is an autocrat not subject to such procedures and accountability. Demosthenes made this critical point in his speech *On the Crown*, a look back nearly ten years after Chaeronea at the events and mistakes that led to that disaster. As an autocrat, Philip "did whatever he wished. He did not announce his intentions in official decrees, did not deliberate in public, was not hauled into court by sycophants, was not prosecuted for moving illegal proposals, was not accountable to anyone. In short, he was ruler, commander, in control of everything."[91] In contrast, as Demosthenes had said even before Chaeronea, the Athenians are "forever debating the same question and never making any progress," passing "empty decrees," and indulging the "hopes of the [speaker's] platform." In another speech, he explicitly identified the danger of verbal procedure substituting for timely action. "All words, apart from action, seem vain and idle, especially from Athenian lips: for the greater our reputation for a ready tongue, the greater the distrust it inspires in all men."[92] Public deliberation, the danger of demagogic rhetoric, and excesses of formal accountability all made it easier for the citizens to substitute words for deed, and thus to avoid the personal service and expense of challenging an aggressor.

After the mid-fourth century, enthusiasm for personal military service indeed declined among Athenians, who relied instead on mercenaries. Demosthenes tried to warn his fellow citizens of the dangers that come from putting their security and interests in the hands of hired professionals. In 351, he told the Athenians, "I propose that you should get ready a corps to carry on a continuous war of annoyance against Philip. Not an imposing army—on paper—of ten or twenty thousand mercenaries! It shall be a real Athenian contingent, and whether you appoint one general or more . . . him it shall strictly follow and obey."[93]

---

91. Demosthenes 18.235, trans. Vince.
92. Demosthenes 4.33–34, 45; 2.12, trans. Vince.
93. Demosthenes 4.19–20, trans. Vince.

Mercenaries obviously have interests quite different from those of the citizens, mainly getting paid, and when their pay is not forthcoming, frequently use their power to acquire payment even if they compromise the interests of those who hire them. The mercenaries Athens had hired, their pay in arrears, had set about attacking and plundering Athens's allies. Thus Athenian soldiers and generals were necessary to oversee and control the hired soldiers.

The Athenian habit of withholding pay from mercenaries points to Demosthenes's other criticism of his fellow citizens in the years leading up to Chaeronea—their unwillingness to forgo some of their state money in order to adequately fund a response to Philip's aggression: "We refuse to pay war-taxes or to serve in person; we cannot keep our hands off the public funds," Demosthenes complained in 341. In another speech that same year, Demosthenes pleaded, "We must make provision for defense, I mean with war-galleys, funds, and men; for even if all other states succumb to slavery, we surely must fight the battle of liberty."[94] Earlier in 349, he told the Athenians they had enough funds for financing the military, "But you appropriate it for yourselves, to suit yourselves."[95] At issue at this time was the theoric fund discussed above, which paid Athenians to attend religious festivals including the theater. The year before Demosthenes's speech a citizen named Apollodorus had proposed that the Athenians vote on whether surplus revenues should go into the military fund. The proposal passed, but Apollodorus subsequently was fined 15 talents. After that, a law was passed that made such a transfer a capital crime. It wasn't until the eve of Chaeronea that a law was passed that transferred the theoric money into the military fund.

Demosthenes's speeches of this period can be faulted for exaggeration and partisan self-interest. But they touch on a fundamental criticism of the radical democracy: that personal self-interest and entitlement transfers will take precedence over military preparedness and action. The historian Pompeius Trogus, writing in the time of the Roman Emperor Augustus, linked this decadence to the defeat of Athens by

---

94. Demosthenes 9.70–71, trans. Vince.
95. Demosthenes 3.11, trans. Vince.

Philip: the Athenians having "fallen into indolence and sloth," the "state revenues they had once spent on the army and the fleet were devoted instead to holidays and festivals. . . . It was then that the public treasury, which had been used to support the soldiers and sailors, began to be divided among the people in the city. In this way it happened that in a Greece preoccupied with entertainment the previously lowly and obscure name of Macedon was able to emerge."[96] In the end, Athens lost its political freedom and autonomy, both of which were never regained in antiquity.

The Excesses of Freedom and Equality

The most important innovation of constitutional government is the idea of political freedom and citizen equality. Unlike the kingdoms and empires of the ancient Mediterranean, where only kings or elites enjoyed full freedom as the perquisite of their status or class, the city-states of Greece predicated freedom on the political institutions and offices in which power resided: thus "the state is a community of free-men," as Aristotle writes, with equal citizen access to the institutions of power.[97] The Greeks explicitly defined themselves in terms of political freedom, in contrast to their non-Greek neighbors who lived in subjection to kings and various elites. The Persians, twice defeated in battle by the free Greeks, particularly embodied the slavishness of the politically subjected, who had to bow down before the Great King and kiss the ground. In contrast, as the Spartan Demaratus told Xerxes during his invasion of Greece in 480, although the Spartans "are free, they're not entirely free: their master is the law, and they're far more afraid of this than your men are of you."[98] Citizens are free because by the laws that transcend any one man, they have the right to participate in freely deliberating policy and governing the state.

---

96. From the epitome of Justin, in Jennifer Tolbert Roberts, *Athens on Trial* (Princeton, 1994), 108.
97. *Politics* 1279a, trans. Jowett.
98. Herodotus 7.104, trans. Waterfield.

To many critics of ancient Athens, however, this ideal of ordered liberty for citizens dependent on law was corrupted into personal license by the masses incapable of understanding properly the true purpose of political freedom: not to live as one likes, but to live a collective life suitable for a rational and virtuous human being, in a state whose aim is to achieve "excellence," as Aristotle writes, and "to make the citizens good and just."[99] According to Thucydides at least, Pericles himself in his Funeral Oration in contrast extols the fact that in Athens, "we do not feel called upon to be angry with our neighbor for doing what he likes," for "we live exactly as we please." Later in Thucydides, when Nicias is exhorting his men before a critical naval engagement at Syracuse, he reminds them "of their country, the freest of the free, and of the unfettered discretion allowed to all in it to live as they pleased."[100] Aristotle agreed with this salient feature of democracy: since "the basis of a democratic state is liberty," an important principle is "that a man should live as he likes."[101] To critics, however, this freedom joined to political power led to the corruption of the state by the zero-sum, centrifugal forces of clashing preferences, passions, and aims among the citizens.

Plato is particularly severe on the personal freedom that characterizes democracies, given that the mass of men are driven by their bodily appetites and passions, indulgence of which compromises the true freedom produced by living rationally and virtuously "according to the rule of the constitution," as Aristotle says in rejecting democracy's belief that "freedom means doing what one likes."[102] In the *Republic* Plato has Socrates describe Democratic Man as a creature of disorderly license: "Are they not free," he asks rhetorically of the denizens of democracy, "and is not the city full of freedom and frankness—a man may say and do what he likes . . . [and] the individual is clearly able to order for himself his own life as he pleases?" This selfish freedom, moreover, leaves the people indifferent to the virtues of their leaders, "never giving a

---

99. *Politics* 1280b, trans. Jowett.
100. Thucydides 2.37, 39; 7.69, trans. Crawley.
101. *Politics* 1317b, trans. Jowett.
102. *Politics* 1310a, trans. Jowett.

thought to the pursuits which make a statesman, and promoting to honour any one who professes to be the people's friend," in the end creating a "charming form of government, full of variety and disorder."[103] The consequence, however, is the corruption of the citizens, who call "anarchy liberty, and waste magnificence, and impudence courage," and give themselves over to "the freedom and libertinism of useless and unnecessary pleasures."[104] Hierarchical distinctions of authority between citizens and aliens, fathers and children, husbands and wives, and free men and slaves all break down to the point that even the "horses and asses have a way of marching along with all the rights and dignities of freemen; and they will run at any body who comes in their way if he does not leave the road clear for them: and all things are just ready to burst with liberty." Eventually, the people, "drunk on the wine of freedom," will sell their liberty to any tyrant who promises to continue to indulge their appetites and passions.[105] For as Aristotle says of this process, "most persons would rather live in a disorderly than in a sober manner."[106]

Just as political freedom degenerates into destructive license, democratic equality is transformed into radical egalitarianism—in Plato's satiric exaggeration above, one including even animals. In Athens equality was codified in the equal access to offices, the courts, and the Assembly: "For if liberty and equality are chiefly to be found in democracy," writes Aristotle, "they will be best attained when all persons alike share in the government to the utmost."[107] But this equality of governing creates dissatisfaction with the inequalities of wealth, talent, or even luck that naturally distinguish men from each other, and it encourages efforts to eliminate or lessen these inequalities. Aristotle makes this dynamic a defining attribute of democracy, which "arises out of the notion that those who are equal in any respect are equal in all respects; because men

---

103. *Republic* 557b–58c, trans. Jowett.
104. *Republic* 560e–61c, trans. Jowett.
105. *Republic* 562c–63c, trans. Jowett.
106. *Politics* 1319b, trans. Jowett.
107. *Politics* 1291b, trans. Jowett.

are equally free, they claim to be absolutely equal."[108] Hence the use of the lottery, as Plato points out, to assign honors and offices and to "give even results in the distributions."[109] But this egalitarianism is contrary to the reality of human nature and abilities. It is an unjust "numerical" equality inferior to "proportional" equality, which Plato says "dispenses more to the greater and less to the smaller, giving due measure to each according to nature; and with regard to honors also, by granting the greater to those that are greater in goodness, and the less to those of the opposite character in respect of goodness and education, it assigns in proportion what is fitting to each. Indeed, it is precisely this which constitutes for us 'political justice.' "[110]

Thus the fundamental danger of democracy in the eyes of its critics, the redistribution of property, arises from this need to eliminate the most obvious sign of inequality, that of wealth, leading to civil war and revolution. That is why the Athenian Stranger in Plato's *Laws*, whose criticisms of "numerical" equality were quoted above, concedes that in his ideal state it may be necessary "to employ even this equality in a modified degree, if [the state] is to avoid involving itself in intestine discord."[111] So too Aristotle, for whom "the equalization of property is one of the things that tend to prevent citizens from quarrelling."[112] In 391 Aristophanes comically dramatized the dangers of such equalization in *Women at Assembly*. In the play a conspiracy of Athenian women take control of the Assembly and pass legislation calling for a radical equalization of property. The ringleader Praxagora proposes a motion "that everyone ought to go shares and hold all things in common / And live on that basis. It's wrong for one man to be rich and another a pauper."[113] Aristophanes shows the absurdity of such equalization as the law expands beyond property to

---

108. *Politics* 1301a, trans. Jowett.
109. *Laws* 757b, trans. R. G. Bury. *Plato: Laws Books 1–6*. Cambridge and London, 1926. Cf. *Republic* 558c.
110. *Laws* 757c, trans. Bury.
111. *Laws* 757d, trans. Bury.
112. *Politics* 1267a, trans. Jowett.
113. *Women at Assembly* 590–91, trans. Douglas N. MacDowell, in *Aristophanes and Athens* (Oxford, 1995), 313.

include sexual partners, who will be enjoyed in common, the ugly men and women getting first dibs on the attractive. In the real world, given human nature and its self-interested greed, schemes of redistribution and collective ownership will end up in either revolution or civil discord.

The Antidemocratic Tradition

This city is free, and ruled by no one man.
The people reign, in annual succession.
They do not yield the power to the rich;
The poor man has an equal share in it.

—Euripides, *The Suppliant Women*[114]

This portrait of ancient Athens and the flaws of democracy is, of course, one-sided and historically simplistic. Partly this bias reflects the accident of textual survival: few pro-democratic works are extant that counterbalance those of the critics. But there are champions of Athenian democracy, none more famous than Pericles in his Funeral Oration. Nor should we ever forget that the Athens of its harshest critics was also the Athens of Marathon, Salamis, the Parthenon, Sophocles, Plato, Socrates, Aristophanes, Thucydides, and the best of ancient philosophy—the city of free speech, citizen autonomy, and an open society. And for all their excesses and flaws, we are all indebted to the notions of political freedom and equality apart from wealth and birth that first appear in ancient Athens.

In fact, many of the objections to mass-rule outlined above were answered by ancient writers. For example, the philosopher Protagoras, in the Platonic dialogue of the same name, counters the charge that the average man is incapable of ruling because he lacks specialized knowledge. Humans could not live peacefully in cities, Protagoras argues in his myth of the origins of politics, had not Zeus granted them "reverence and justice to be the ordering principles of cities and the bonds of friendship and conciliation." When asked by Hermes whether these vir-

---

114. Euripides, *The Suppliant Women*, 404–7, trans. Jones.

tues and skills should be distributed like the skills of crafts to the few, Zeus responds, "I should like them all to have a share; for cities cannot exist, if a few only share in the virtues, as in the arts." Thus, Protagoras concludes, when the citizens "meet to deliberate about political virtues, which proceeds only by way of justice and wisdom, they are patient enough of any man who speaks to them, as is also natural, because they think that every man ought to share in this sort of virtue, and that states could not exist if this were otherwise."[115]

Similarly, Aristotle, who as we have seen was no great friend of "extreme" democracy, questions the notion that the masses when they deliberate will end up being driven by self-interest and passion because they lack virtue and wisdom. "For the many, of whom each individual is not a good man, when they meet together may be better than the few good, if regarded not individually but collectively. . . . For each individual among the many has a share of excellence and practical wisdom, and when they meet together, just as they become in a manner one man, who has many feet, and hands, and senses, so too with regard to their character and thought." Thus, "although individually they [the masses] may be worse judges than those who have special knowledge, as a body they are as good or better." Aristotle applies this principle regarding the courts to the Assembly and Council as well.[116] As for the disorders and injustice with which critics charge democracies, Herodotus puts in the mouth of the Persian Otanes the answer to this charge, praising "equality before the law" and "accountable government" as the cures for the "vices of monarchy," the tyranny and disorder that ensue "when a monarch has the license to do whatever he wants, without being accountable to anyone."[117] For every excessive vice documented by the critics of democracy, there is a virtue, and for every flaw, a strength.

Historian David Stockton is right, then, to remind us, in response to the critics, of the Athenians' "attitude to life, the very air of individuality,

---

115. *Protagoras* 322c–23a, trans. Jowett, *The Dialogues of Plato*, vol. 1.
116. *Politics* 1281b–82a, trans. Jowett. Thucydides (6.39) puts the same sentiment in the mouth of the Syracusan Athenagoras.
117. *Histories* 3.8, trans. Waterfield.

open-mindedness, and independence which they breathe, the excitement and novelty (and, implicitly, the fragility) of this great experiment in participation and equality" as expressed in Pericles's Funeral Oration, which "in its eloquent advocacy of the virtues of 'government of the people, by the people, and for the people' . . . was the earliest, and for many readers remains the finest, statement of what a democracy should aspire to be."[118]

Yet in subsequent ages, the antidemocratic tradition had more influence on political theorists than did the virtues and achievements of Athens. The subjection of her fellow Greeks to the empire, the folly of the Sicilian Expedition, and the definitive failure to defend her freedom from Philip II of Macedon all weighed more in the balance. For the American colonists who set about framing a structure of government after the Revolution, the flaws and failures of Athens and radical democracy, documented by brilliant writers like Thucydides, Plato, and Aristotle, were powerful warnings of mistakes to avoid.

---

118. In *The Classical Athenian Democracy* (Oxford, 1990), 186–87.

CHAPTER TWO

The Antidemocratic Tradition
and the American Founding

Sobriety, abstinence, and *severity,* were never remarkable characteristics of democracy, or the democratical branch or mixture, in any constitution; they have oftener been the attributes of aristocracy and oligarchy. Athens, in particular, was never conspicuous for these qualities; but, on the contrary, from the first to the last moments of her democratical constitution, *levity, gayety, inconstancy, dissipation, intemperance, debauchery,* and a *dissolution of manners,* were the prevailing character of the whole nation.

—John Adams, *A Defense of the Constitutions of Government of the United States of America*[1]

A democracy is a volcano, which conceals the fiery elements of its own destruction. These will produce an eruption, and carry desolation in their way.

—Fisher Ames[2]

Given that colonial America's schools were steeped in the literature, history, and philosophy of ancient Greece and Rome, Americans of the late eighteenth century were intimately familiar with the follies and failures of Athenian democracy, as well as the two millennia of commentary on them. For the less formally educated, theatrical productions, public orations, and newspapers "familiarized American audiences with

---

1. *The Works of John Adams,* vol. 6, ed. Charles Francis Adams (Boston, 1851), 100–1. Unless otherwise noted, emphases in quotations below are the authors'.
2. Massachusetts Federal Constitution ratifying convention, January 1788. In *The Debate on the Constitution,* vol. 1, ed. Bernard Bailyn (New York, 1993), 894.

classical lore and republican ideals," as Forrest McDonald writes.[3] The
classical influence was particularly important for the political thinking
of those who would craft the new nation's political order. "The classics,"
historian Carl J. Richard writes, "supplied mixed government theory,
the principal basis for the US Constitution. The classics contributed a
great deal to the founders' conception of human nature, their understanding of the nature and purpose of virtue, and their appreciation of
society's essential role in its production. . . . In short, the classics supplied
a large portion of the founders' intellectual tools."[4] These influences,
moreover, were as much negative as positive, a record of the political follies and vices of a human nature constant over space and time. "Similar
causes," Antifederalist Benjamin Austin said in 1778, "will forever operate like effects in the political, moral, and physical world: those vices
which ruined the illustrious republics of Greece, and the mighty commonwealth of Rome . . . must eventually overturn every state, where their
deleterious influence is suffered to prevail."[5]

This tradition comprised not just the Greek writers like Thucydides,
Plato, and Aristotle, whom the founders formally studied, but also later
Roman and Continental political philosophers and theorists. Like the
Greek critics, these political writers distrusted a common people whom
they deemed to be afflicted with ignorance and self-interest, and thus
vulnerable to the machinations of ambitious demagogues and politicians.
In the Roman orator Cicero's *Pro Flacco*, Americans could learn that
Athens collapsed because of "one evil, the immoderate liberty and licentiousness of the popular assemblies. When inexperienced men, ignorant
and uninstructed in any description of business whatever, took their seats
in the theatre, then they undertook inexpedient wars; then they appointed
seditious men to the government of the republic; then they banished from
the city the citizens who had deserved best of the state."[6] The second-

---

3. *Novus Ordo Seclorum* (Lawrence, KS, 1985), 69.
4. *The Founders and the Classics* (Cambridge, MA, 1994), 8.
5. In Gordon S. Wood, *The Creation of the American Republic* (1969; Chapel
   Hill and London, 1998), 52.
6. *Pro Flacco* 16. In *The Orations of Marcus Tullius Cicero*, trans. C. D. Yonge
   (Covent Garden, 1856).

century AD historian Plutarch, the most-read ancient writer in early America, reprised in his paired biographies of eminent Greeks and Romans and in other writings the earlier criticisms of Athens, especially of the masses who were "shifting and changeable as the winds," who "always smile upon him who gives to them and does them favours," and among whom exist "a spirit of malice and fault-finding directed against men in public life."[7] In the sixteenth century, political theorist Thomas Elyot called the Athenian masses a "monster with many heads," and Walter Raleigh in the seventeenth century scorned them as the "rascal multitude."[8] In the introduction to his influential translation of Thucydides in 1629, Thomas Hobbes wrote of the Athenians that "wicked men and flatterers drave [sic] them headlong into those actions that were to ruin them," repeating the common charge that the ignorant, self-interested masses are vulnerable to demagogues.[9] Another important influence on the founders, James Harrington's *Oceana* (1656), repeated the Socratic and Aristotlean charge that the unlettered laboring masses have no time to acquire the virtue and knowledge necessary for guiding the state: "mechanics, until they have first feathered their nests—like the fowls of the air, whose sole employment is to seek their food—are so busied in their private concernments that they have no leisure" for studying the political philosophy knowledge of which, in the antidemocratic tradition, is crucial for managing government.[10]

Democracy—a government in which the preponderance of power is vested in the assemblies of the people rather than in representatives or executives not directly accountable to the people—did have its champions in the decades before the Founding. Supporters of popular rule were found in the North among the small towns and farms beyond the mercantile cities. There agrarian traditions of self-sufficiency and self-reliance, preference for home rule and the annual rotation of office-

---

7. *Pericles* 15.2; *Praecepta Rei Publicae Gerendae* 821F, 813A, in Roberts, *Athens on Trial*, 334 n. 29; 335 n. 30.
8. In the *Boke Named the Governour* 1.10, in Roberts, 138; Raleigh, *History of the World*, in Roberts, 142.
9. Roberts, 143.
10. Roberts, 145.

holders, and suspicion of the corrupting concentration of power distant from the watchful eyes of the citizens, all made a more direct democracy the desired form of government. An anonymous pamphlet printed in 1776, *The People the Best Governor*, argued, as one would expect from the title, "The people know best their own wants and necessities, and therefore are best able to rule themselves."[11] In 1778 the town of Westminster, Massachusetts, resolved, "The oftener power Returns into the hands of the people the Better . . . Where can the power be lodged so Safe as in the Hands of the people and who can Delligate [sic] it So Well as they, or who has the boldness without Blushing to Say that the people are not Suitable to putt [sic] in their own officers?"[12] This preference for democracy—though not quite as "extreme" as ancient Athens's—formed the nucleus of the Antifederalist opposition to the Constitutional Convention of 1787, whose delegates in the estimation of some Antifederalists were a "monstrous aristocracy" that would "swallow up the democratic rights of the union, and sacrifice the liberties of the people to the power and domination of the few," as a commentator calling himself "Rusticus" said.[13] Patrick Henry put it more bluntly: "The tyranny of Philadelphia may be like the tyranny of George III."[14]

But the radical state governments that sprang up between the Declaration of Independence and the Constitutional Convention that convened in late May 1787, validated for many the traditional antidemocratic sentiments and prejudices. Pennsylvania's Constitution was particularly extreme, with its unicameral legislature, annual elections, wider suffrage rights, Council of Censors to ensure fealty to the constitution, and elimination of property qualifications for assemblymen. They also created a Supreme Executive Council, one-third of whose members were replaced yearly, on the principle that, as Antifederalist writer James Burgh put it, "Where annual elections end, slavery begins." As historian David Lefer writes, it "was probably the closest attempt at direct democ-

---

11. In Bernard Bailyn, *The Ideological Origins of the American Revolution* (Cambridge, MA, 1967), 294.
12. In *The Antifederalists*, Jackson Turner Main (1961; New York, 1974), 14.
13. In *The Antifederalists*, 134.
14. In Wood, 521.

racy since the days of Pericles." Other provisions, moreover, confirmed the antidemocratic suspicions and fears of extreme democracy. The constitution abolished debtors' prisons and contemplated laws, rejected by a slim margin, to discourage concentrations of wealth. Pennsylvanian physician Benjamin Rush called Pennsylvania's government a "mobocracy," an English translation of the third-century Greek historian Polybius's word *ochlokratia*, used to describe a degenerate democracy.[15] According to Dr. Rush, his friend John Minton hated the constitution and feared its malign influences so much that he suffered from "political hypochondriases which put an end to his life."[16] Equally worrisome to antidemocrats, Vermont and Georgia adopted similar constitutions, and radical democrats in other states attempted to do likewise.

The threat of violence from the intemperate mob predicted by ancient critics of democracy seemingly became a reality in Pennsylvania. In May 1779, unsuccessful efforts by conservatives to call another constitutional convention, economic hard times, and runaway inflation sparked violence against shopkeepers accused of manipulating prices. "Merchants found guilty [of overpricing]," Lefer writes, "were summarily hauled from their shops and marched through town. Many were beaten and several thrown in prison. Warehouses and homes were invaded, ships seized, and private property impounded." Committees were formed to control prices and pursue those who violated their laws. The violence intensified throughout the summer, and in October, a mob kidnapped four merchants and attacked the house of lawyer James Wilson, an outspoken critic of the constitution and a future Supreme Court justice. Wilson and thirty others fortified the house, shots were exchanged, and in a few minutes five men were dead. Equally ominous, the radicals took full control of the assembly in an election held one week after the violence. Henry Laurens wrote to John Adams, "We are at this moment on a precipice, and what I have

---

15. *The Founding Conservatives* (New York, 2013), 135, 138.
16. In Chilton Williamson, *American Suffrage from Property to Democracy* (Princeton, NJ, 1960), 99.

long dreaded . . . seems to be breaking forth—a convulsion among the people."[17]

The Fort Wilson Riot, as it became known, for antidemocrats was graphic evidence of the wages of extreme democracy. But Shays' Rebellion, which unfolded over the nine months before the convention convened in May 1787, had more immediate impact. Two thousand mostly small farmers of central and western Massachusetts, protesting against debt and high taxes, shut down the courts to prevent judicial proceedings for tax and debt collection, and eventually formed a militia that marched on the federal armory in Springfield. The rebels were suppressed, in part by a private army funded by the well to do. This incident gave even more traction to the old antidemocratic charges that more power to the people meant attacks on property, forgiveness of debt, and violent anarchy. David Humphreys, one of George Washington's aides-de-camp during the Revolutionary War and a member of the Connecticut state legislature, blamed the uprising on "a licentious spirit prevailing among many of the people; a leveling principle; a desire for change."[18]

The solution to this alleged populist anarchy and rage for the redistribution of property and cancellation of debt was a national government stronger than that of the Articles of Confederation. In 1786, Revolutionary War hero General Henry Knox wrote to George Washington concerning Shays' Rebellion, "On the very first impression of faction and licentiousness, the fine theoretic government of Massachusetts has given way." The rebels, Knox claims, "have never paid any, or but very little taxes—But they see the weakness of government; They feel at once their own poverty, compared with the opulent, and their own force, and they are determined to make use of the latter, in order to remedy the former." Private property, having been protected from England by the Revolution, as Knox interprets the rebels' motives, "'therefore ought to be the common property of all. And he that attempts opposition to this creed is an enemy of equity and justice.' . . . In a word they are determined to annihilate all debts public and private." He con-

---

17. *The Founding Conservatives*, 216, 219–25.
18. In *The Antifederalists*, 62.

cludes, "What is to give us security against the violence of lawless men? Our government must be braced, changed, or altered to secure our lives and property."[19]

Shays' Rebellion, which took place closer to the convention, was a more immediate example of the disorder fomented in the postwar years by overly democratic state governments and the misguided, short-sighted, easily manipulated common people who, according to future Congressman Fisher Ames in 1787, "themselves have, in almost every instance, been the ready instruments of their own ruin," allowing themselves to become the prey to "blustering, haughty, licentious, self-seeking men."[20] During this period many of the other disparaging attacks on the people familiar from the ancient critics surveyed above were common in political writing. The rise of "new men," who in the turbulence of the Revolution began taking positions of power, elicited from James Otis— the Massachusetts lawyer who said, "Taxation without representation is tyranny"—an insult redolent of the aristocrat Theognis: "When the pot boils, the scum will rise." A New Yorker calling himself "Sober Citizen" similarly complained of the novel prominence of parvenus and vulgar upstarts *"whose fathers they* [more respectable men] *would have disdained to have sat with the dogs of their flocks,"* but who now have been "raised to immense wealth." The Socratic scorn for the "tinkers and cobblers" presuming to be statesmen was reprised by a Baltimore printer who snorted, "When a man, who is only fit 'to patch a shoe,' attempts 'to patch the State,' fancies himself a *Solon* or *Lycurgus* . . . he cannot fail to meet with contempt." The penchant of members of democratic assemblies to be manipulated by the ambitious was noted in a letter published in the *Providence Gazette* complaining that "a set of unprincipled men, who sacrifice everything to their popularity and private views, seem to have acquired too much influence in our Assemblies." And just as many ancient critics saw eternal class warfare between the rich elites and the poor masses, an article in the *Pennsylvania Journal* agreed, albeit

---

19. In W. W. Abbot and Dorothy Twohig, eds. *The Papers of George Washington: Confederation Series*, vol. 4 (Charlottesville, 1983), 300.
20. In Wood, 397.

from the democratical side: "All political societies have two contending parties—the majority, whose interest it is to be free, and who have the power to be so—and the minority, whose interest it is to oppress, but who can never succeed, till they have blinded their opponents."[21]

Seemingly confirmed in the turbulent years after the break from England, the antidemocratic tradition—to be sure, as biased and one-sided in early America as it was in ancient Athens—with its fear of "extreme democracy" and its distrust of the political empowerment of the masses, was a powerful and decisive influence on the political philosophy of the late eighteenth century and the crafting of the Constitution.

The Distrust of Human Nature

Like the Athenian critics of democracy, Colonial era antidemocrats assumed that men in the mass were dangerous in part because of the eternal flaws of human nature. Americans of that time obtained this pessimistic view of people from both their Classical and Christian heritages. The tragic vision evident in Greek literature from Thucydides to tragedians like Sophocles and Euripides defined humans as hostages to time, unforeseen change, a harsh natural world, the capricious gods, and the destructive powers of their own appetites and passions.

In most men reason is helpless against these forces, and more often than not will be corrupted by the passions in order to serve their ends. Nor can the power of the irrational over human behavior be eliminated or even diminished by improvement, for it is foundational to human identity. In Thucydides's history, an irrational human nature constant over space and time is the key to understanding social and political behavior, particularly the causes and conduct of wars and civil strife. In his description of the horrors of revolution in Corcyra in 427 BC, Thucydides famously articulated his unsparing realism in a passage John Adams quotes at length in his *Defense of the Constitutions*: "The sufferings which revolution entailed upon the cities were many and terri-

---

21. In Wood, 476, 477, 476–77, 478, 503.

ble, such as have occurred and always will occur as long as the nature of mankind remains the same," for war confronts people with "imperious necessities" and "so proves a rough master that brings most men's characters to a level with their fortunes."[22]

Similarly, Christianity's doctrine of man's fallen nature and the necessity of God's grace to achieve redemption put out of bounds the notion that the improvement of reason without divine aid, and the secular expansion of knowledge, could eliminate or temper for long the destructive irrationalism of human nature. America's most important theologian of the eighteenth century, Jonathan Edwards, wrote that "the *innate sinful depravity of the* heart," the "universal unfailing tendency to that moral evil," the "state of man's nature, that disposition of the mind, is to be looked upon as evil and pernicious, which, as it is in itself, tends to extremely pernicious consequences."[23] Edwards especially highlights the bloody record of history, in which the perennial violence and cruelty of man against his fellows proves his innate depravity.

Nor can we dismiss Edwards's views as the consequence of his grim Calvinism. The titan of the Enlightenment, Voltaire, in 1769 expressed the same pessimism about human nature: "Men in general are foolish, ungrateful, jealous, covetous of their neighbor's goods. . . . Power is commonly possessed, in States and in families, by those who have the strongest arms, the most resolute minds, and the hardest hearts. From which the moralists of all ages have concluded that the human species is of little worth."[24] Indeed, for most thinkers of the eighteenth century, including the intellectual milieu of many of the founders, the improvement of human nature in the mass was out of the question. On the con-

22. Thucydides 3.82, trans. Crawley; Adams, *Works*, vol. 4, 285.
23. *The Great Christian Doctrine of Original Sin Defended*, 8, http://www.prayer meetings.org/files/Jonathan_Edwards/JE_The_Great_Christian_Doctrine _Of_Original_Sin_Defended.pdf.
24. *Dieu et les hommes*, in Arthur O. Lovejoy, *Reflections on Human Nature* (Baltimore, MD, 1961), 6. Voltaire, of course, was more optimistic about the possibility of some level of improvement through reducing religious superstition and ignorance by an increase of knowledge and the cultivation of reason.

trary, the theorists of the Constitution followed the "just *political* maxim" of English philosopher David Hume, *"that every man must be supposed a knave."*[25] A more just and equitable political order had to be constructed out of this unpromising material, taking it into account rather than wishing it away.

Particularly in the disorderly decade between the Declaration of Independence and the Constitutional Convention, the selfish interests and destructive passions of the bulk of men are continually highlighted as the fatal flaw of democracy. As we saw earlier, the democratic excesses of some of the state governments in this period that vested the bulk of governing power in popularly elected legislatures sharpened this criticism. As one historian writes, "Colonial electors were notoriously volatile: they had turned out to vote only intermittently and only on issues about which they had strong emotions." The result was legislation passed with "too hasty, careless, incautious and passionate proceedings; breaches of wholesome order and necessary form," as "A Democratic Federalist" wrote in 1787.[26] New York's Trespass Act of 1783, which gave American patriots the right to sue loyalists who had damaged or occupied property left behind British lines during the war, violated common law, natural law, and the Anglo-American legal tradition.[27] And it was wildly popular. To many antidemocrats, such attacks on the property rights of loyalists, schemes to distribute public lands, and inflationary economic policies that devalued debts all smacked of the redistribution of property and relief of debt that ancient critics warned would follow from giving the common people too much power. During Shays' Rebellion, one citizen worried that the rebels' demands "must end in an abolition of all public & private debts and then an equal distribution of Property may be demanded."[28] Such critics reprised the old charges we surveyed in the previous chapter: the masses are moti-

---

25. In Rahe, *Republics Ancient and Modern*, vol. 3, 45.
26. Alison G. Olson, "Thoughts on Why America Chose a Congressional Rather Than a Parliamentary Form of Government," in *Inventing Congress*, eds. Kenneth R. Bowling and Donald R. Kennon (Athens, OH, 1999), 36.
27. McDonald, 156–57.
28. In Main, *The Antifederalists*, 105.

vated by passions, class envy, and self-interest, ignorant of the knowledge necessary for forming policy, and as such are prey to ambitious, manipulative demagogues who will make the people dupes for advancing self-serving policies dangerous for the state as a whole; as Alexander Addison of Pennsylvania put it, "To mislead the judgment of the people, where they have *all* the power, must produce the greatest possible mischief."[29]

Such low opinions of the masses were ubiquitous in the years before the convention. Responding to Thomas Paine's *Common Sense* (1776) and its championing of greater power for the people, critics called up the usual dangers antidemocrats had decried for over two millennia. John Adams, the most prolific and eloquent critic of unchecked democracy, complained that Paine's planned government with its unicameral legislature "was so democratical, without any restraint or even an attempt at any equilibrium or counterpoise, that it must produce confusion and every evil work."[30] Charles Inglis warned, "All our property throughout the continent would be unhinged," and "the greatest confusion, and the most violent convulsions would take place." Another critic, James Chalmers, conjured the specter of debt cancellation, the evil twin of property redistribution: "A war will ensue between the creditors and their debtors, which will eventually end in a general spunge [sic] or abolition of debts, which has more than once happened in other states on occasions similar." Paine's suggestions could be taken seriously only if he could assure his fellow colonists "that ambition, pride, avarice, and all that dark train of the passions which attend them" did not exist in Americans. The ubiquity of human depravity demonstrated on every page of history meant that no such assurances could be given for the people as a whole. On the contrary, as Virginian Carter Braxton wrote, "A disinterested attachment to the public good, exclusive and independent of all private and selfish interest" had "never characterized the mass of people in any state."[31]

---

29. In McDonald, 49.
30. In Bailyn, 286–87.
31. In Wood, 94–95, 96.

Checking the excesses of the *demos* thus was a critical goal in the construction of the new political order. It was important to avoid giving too much power to "Men without Character and without Fortune," as Edward Rutledge wrote to John Jay, and thus avoid a government "managed by the *promiscuous multitude of the community*," a New Jersey reader proclaimed in the *New Jersey Gazette*. The "multitude" might be honest, he continued, "yet from many natural defects, are generally in the execution of government, violent, changeable, and liable to many fatal errors." John Adams remarked on the ignorance of the people as the impediment to their responsible and disinterested exercise of power, for "few of them [are] much read in the history, laws, or politics, even of their own, not to mention other states, from whose rises, revolutions and declensions the great landmarks of legislations and government are taken." As in the ancient critics, the fickleness, self-interest, and ignorance of the people made them vulnerable to "*demagogues*" who "under plausible pretenses [sic], . . . for dark, ambitious, or (not unlikely) speculative purposes, which they dare not own," were "disturbing the peace of the public, and causing the government to be bullied." If left unchecked, popular governments would lead to tyranny, for as South Carolinian Aedanus Burke orated, "a popular assembly not governed by fundamental laws, but under the bias of anger, malice, or a thirst for revenge, will commit more excess than an arbitrary monarch."[32]

Moreover, the solution of some ancient antidemocrats for avoiding the weaknesses of the masses—reserving power for an elite superior because of virtue, blood, or wisdom—in the eighteenth century was obviated by the belief that human depravity was a universal evil irrespective of birth or education; that, as John Locke said, "We are all centaurs and tis the beast that carrys [sic] us."[33] As such, most people, even those of virtue and wisdom, could not be trusted for long with unchecked power, for power gave them the ability to act on their irrational passions and destructive impulses at the expense of the community. Even the elitist aristocrat Plato warned, "If any one gives too great

---

32. In Wood, 204–5, 209, 369, 405.
33. In Rahe, *Republics Ancient and Modern*, vol. 2, 226.

a power to anything . . . and does not observe the mean, everything is overthrown, and, in the wantonness of excess runs in the one case to disorders, and in the other to injustice, which is the child of excess."[34] Eventually even the virtuous with excessive power will create tyranny, "that arbitrary power of an individual which is responsible to no one, and governs all alike, whether equals or betters, with a view to its own advantage, not to that of its subjects," as Aristotle defined it.[35] Such a description is consistent with the claim in the Declaration of Independence that British king George III's "history of repeated injuries and usurpations" all had "in direct object the establishment of an absolute Tyranny over these states."

Colonial Americans could find historical models of George III in the oppressive "tyrants" in Classical history and literature, and the many examples of such corruption given scope by power. They could read in Plutarch's *Lives* about tyrants like Julius Caesar, who destroyed the Roman Republic in 46 BC, and examples of resistance to them like Brutus, Cassius, and Cato the Younger, popular pseudonyms for Colonial political commentators. One of the most popular works of literature in this period was Joseph Addison's play *Cato* (1713), which dramatized the last days of Cato. Cato committed suicide rather than submit to the tyrant Julius Caesar, thus becoming a martyr to republican freedom. George Washington had the play performed for the troops during the dark days at Valley Forge, and Patrick Henry's famous "Give me liberty, or give me death" is likely a paraphrase of a line from *Cato*.[36]

The Colonists, then, on the whole agreed with the late seventeenth-century English political philosopher Viscount Bolingbroke: "The love of power is natural, it is insatiable; it is whetted, not cloyed, by possession."[37] Warnings against the corruption of unchecked power are as frequent in the years before the Constitutional Convention as complaints about excessive democracy. In 1776, one Marylander wrote, "all

---

34. *Laws* 691b, trans. Jowett.
35. *Politics* 1295a, trans. Jowett.
36. McDonald, 68–69; 10.
37. In Rahe, vol. 2, 205.

men" are "by nature fond of power" and "unwilling to part with the possession of it." About the same time Benjamin Rush observed, "sovereign power should be watched with a jealous eye. . . . Whether that power is lodged in the hands of one or many, the danger is equally great."[38] Alexander Hamilton, reflecting on the disorder and confusion in government in the years after independence, in 1781 cautioned Americans against the "extreme jealousy of power" unleashed by popular revolutions.[39]

Such commonplace sentiments were as usual best expressed in John Adams's *Defense of the Constitutions* in 1787: "Though we allow benevolence and generous affections to exist in the human breast, yet every moral theorist will admit the selfish passions in the generality of men to be the strongest. There are few who love the public better than themselves, though all may have some affection for the public. . . . Self-interest, private avidity, ambition, and avarice, will exist in every state of society, and under every form of government." No elite, or any form of government in which power is not divided, dispersed, and balanced, will avoid the tyranny of the passions, least of all a democracy. Years later Adams would write, "It is in vain to say that democracy is less vain, less proud, less selfish, less ambitious, or less avaricious than aristocracy or monarchy. It is not true, in fact, and nowhere appears in history. Those passions are the same in all men, under all forms of simple government, and when unchecked, produce the same effects of fraud, violence, and cruelty."[40] Clearly neither a government that concentrated power solely in the one, the few, or the many, could be just and stable given the destructive human passions that defined all people.

Framing the Solution

In the early sixteenth century, Machiavelli wrote, "As all those have shown who have discussed civil institutions, and as every history is full

---

38. Wood, 21, 442.
39. McDonald, *Novus Ordo Seclorum*, 2.
40. *The Works of John Adams*, vol. 6, 57. 484.

of examples, it is necessary to whoever arranges to found a Republic and establish laws in it, to presuppose that all men are bad and that they will use their malignity of mind every time they have the opportunity."[41] The fifty-five delegates who gathered in Philadelphia starting on May 25, 1787, were generally in agreement with Machiavelli's dictum. Their task was to form a government that created political freedom but protected individuals and society from the corruption of power.

For all their diversity of opinion and philosophy, historian Walter A. McDougall writes, "all Federalists believed human nature was flawed . . . envisioned no utopias, put little trust in republican virtue, and believed the only government liable to endure was one taking mankind as it was and making allowance for passion and greed."[42] Throughout the Constitutional convention, the delegates repeatedly prefaced their remarks with reminders of the irrational springs of human behavior. Typical are the comments of Benjamin Franklin that were read at the convention during the deliberations about compensation for the president. "There are two passions which have a powerful influence on the affairs of men," Franklin wrote. "These are ambition and avarice; the love of power, and the love of money," which when united have "the most violent effects. . . . The struggles for them [in England] are the true sources of all those factions which are perpetually dividing the Nation, distracting its councils, hurrying sometimes into fruitless & mischievous wars." A power like that of the proposed president, Franklin continues, will attract "the bold and the violent, the men of strong passions and indefatigable activity in their selfish pursuits."[43] Given this tendency for power to corrupt, and money to serve as the instrument of such corrupted power, Franklin argued against compensating the president beyond his expenses.

This belief in a destructive human nature and the distrust of power led most delegates to prefer the mixed government that checked and

---

41. *Discourses*, 1.3, http://www.constitution.org/mac/disclivy1.htm#1:03.
42. *Freedom Just Around the Corner* (New York, 2004), 304.
43. In *The Records of the Federal Convention of 1787*, ed. Max Farrand, rev. ed. (New Haven, CT, 1937), vol. 1, 82.

balanced the power of the people and elites alike. But they particularly distrusted the masses. In the early days of the convention, Edmund Randolph, governor of Virginia, orated, "Our chief danger arises from the democratic parts of our [state] constitutions. It is a maxim which I hold incontrovertible, that the power of government exercised by the people swallows up the other branches. None of the constitutions have provided sufficient checks against the democracy." Elbridge Gerry of Massachusetts agreed with the Southerner: "The evils we experience flow from the excess of democracy. The people do not want virtue; but are the dupes of pretended patriots. In Massts. it has been fully confirmed by experience that they are daily misled into the most baneful measures and opinions by the false reports circulated by designing men" who increased the "danger of the levilling [sic] spirit."[44] As Gordon Wood observes, "The Constitution was intrinsically an aristocratic document designed to check the democratic tendencies of the period."[45] The antidemocratic tradition beginning in ancient Athens found its most significant expression in the creation of the US Constitution.

As such, the Constitution of 1787 was a version of the classical "mixed government" in which the democratical element was confined to the House of Representatives, and the legislative body divided between the House and the Senate. Indeed, given the combined powers of the "monarchical" president and oligarchical Senate, Antifederalist Richard Henry Lee complained that the "democratic branch" of the government was a "mere shred or rag."[46] Some delegates objected to even that level of popularly elected government. Roger Sherman, who had sat on the Committee of Five that drafted the Declaration of Independence, argued against the direct election of the House on the grounds that the people "should have as little to do as may be about the government. They want information and are constantly liable to be misled."[47] In the end, however, the Senate, its members appointed by the state legislatures, was

---

44. Farrand, vol. 1, 26–27, 48.
45. Wood, 513.
46. In Wood, 521.
47. Farrand, vol. 1, 48.

designed in part to check the legislative excesses of the popularly elected House, and Congress itself was subject to the counterbalancing powers of the executive and the judiciary, neither of which was elected by the people. There would be no Athens in America.

Debating the Solution

In the year before the ratification of the Constitution by the necessary nine states on September 13, 1788, opponents and supporters of the new government debated the document both in speeches at the ratifying conventions, and in print even before it was finished. In these contests the argument about democracy and its alleged weaknesses that had appeared in the previous decade were reprised. Many Federalists answered the Antifederalist charge that they were scheming to create some form of aristocracy, by evoking the old antidemocratic specters of mob rule, class warfare, and the dominance of demagogues. Robert Livingstone derided his fellow New Yorker Melancton Smith's worry about dominance by the well-born and the rich by claiming Smith's ideas would lead to a government expressing "the unjust, the selfish, the unsocial feelings," one where "the vices, the infirmities, the passions of the people" would dominate. Federalist Theodore Sedgwick of Massachusetts, a delegate to the Continental Congress and a future senator, considered the Antifederalists to be engaged in class warfare "levied on the virtue, property, and distinctions in the community." Such concerns bespeak how thoroughly engrained in the political consciousness of many Americans was the long tradition of distrust of democracy, and the need to protect, as John Dickinson put it, "the worthy against the licentious."[48]

The most famous of the writings on the Constitution, of course, are those of Alexander Hamilton, John Jay, and James Madison. Their eighty-five articles appeared under the byline Publius in various New York newspapers between October 1787 and August 1788, and were later collected into the book known as *The Federalist*. Throughout these

---

48. In Wood, 293–94, 475.

writings the fundamental assumption behind the problems the framers were confronting, and the solutions they proposed, was the depravity of human nature, as a few examples illustrate.

In *The Federalist* 6, Alexander Hamilton predicated his case for a more powerful central government by arguing the inevitability of conflict and disunion between the states in the absence of a federal counterforce. "A man must be far gone in Utopian speculations," Hamilton wrote, who could doubt that quarrels among the states would lead to "frequent and violent contests with each other. To presume a want of motives for such contests . . . would be to forget that men are ambitious, vindictive and rapacious." Echoing Plato's dictum that war is the natural state of relations among nations, Hamilton points out that "hostilities among nations are innumerable," owing to the "love of power or the desire of preeminence and dominion," and he warns against conflict whose origins lie "in private passions" and "in the attachments, enmities, interests, hopes and fears of leading individuals." Countering the widespread belief, then as today, that commercial nations avoid conflicts because they are damaging to their economic interests, Hamilton responds, "Has it not, on the contrary, invariably been found, that momentary passions and immediate interests have a more active and imperious control over human conduct than general or remote considerations of policy, utility or justice?"[49]

Indeed, it is the passionate and selfish human nature that makes government necessary in the first place. Hamilton asks, "Why has government been instituted at all? Because the passions of men will not conform to the dictates of reason and justice, without constraint." James Madison, in one of the more famous passages from *The Federalist*, agreed. Arguing for the "separate and distinct exercise of the different powers of government," and the ability for each branch "to resist the encroachment of the others," Madison wrote, "Ambition must be made to counteract ambition. The interest of the man must be connected with the constitutional rights of the place. It may be a reflection on human nature, that such

---

49. In *The Federalist*, eds. George W. Carey and James McClellan (Dubuque, IA, 1990), 21, 25. Subsequent references are to this edition.

devices should be necessary to control the abuses of government. But what is government itself but the greatest of all reflections of human nature? If men were angels, no government would be necessary. If angels were to govern men, neither external nor internal controls on government would be necessary."[50]

If government is necessary given human nature, and if "power is of an encroaching nature, and that it ought to be effectually restrained from passing the limits assigned to it," as Madison says, then the structure of government must be such that the natural tendency of power to aggrandize itself at the expense of others will be checked and channeled by dividing power into parts that balance one another. Otherwise, such conflicts of interests will erupt into violent strife and revolution. As John Adams wrote in his *Defense of the Constitutions*, "Human nature is as incapable now of going through revolutions with temper and sobriety, with patience and prudence, or without fury and madness, as it was among the Greeks so long ago. . . . Without three orders, and an effectual balance between them, in every American constitution, it must be destined to frequent unavoidable revolutions."[51]

The justification for representative republic rather than a direct democratical government, one based on the irrational springs of human behavior, finds its most thorough argument in perhaps the most famous article of *The Federalist*. In 10, Madison discusses "faction," "a number of citizens, whether amounting to a majority or minority of the whole, who are united and actuated by some common impulse of passion, or of interest, adverse to the rights of other citizens, or to the permanent and aggregate interests of the community." Given the "passions and interests" that define human nature, a free society gives them scope to a greater number of people: "Liberty is to faction, what air is to fire, an aliment without which it instantly expires." As such, it cannot ever be eliminated from a free human society and politics. "As long as the reason of man continues fallible," Madison continues, "and he is at liberty to exercise it, different opinions will be formed. As long as the connection

50. Hamilton 15, 76; Madison 51, 267.
51. Madison 48, 255; *Works of John Adams*, vol. 4, 297.

subsists between his reason and his self-love, his opinions and his passions will have a reciprocal influence on each other; and the former will be objects to which the latter will attach themselves." The "latent causes of faction are thus sown in the nature of man," and different beliefs about religion or politics, or attachment to ambitious men "have in turn divided mankind into parties, inflamed them with mutual animosity, and rendered them much more disposed to vex and oppress each other, than to cooperate for their common good."[52] Finally, the antidemocratic specter of the redistribution of property and the cancellation of debt haunts Madison's thoughts on faction: "The most common and durable source of factions, has been the various and unequal distribution of property. Those who hold, and those who are without property, have ever formed distinct interests in society. Those who are creditors, and those who are debtors, fall under a like discrimination." How then can freedom be preserved at the same time the ineradicable evils of faction are mitigated?

Madison specifically discounts democratical governments, "which admit of no cure for the mischiefs of faction." Democracy itself, Madison argues, creates a tyranny of the majority that will sacrifice minority interests to its own. "Hence it is, that such Democracies have ever been spectacles of turbulence and contention; have ever been found incompatible with personal security, or the rights of property; and have in general been as short in their lives, as they have been violent in their deaths." The solution is a representative Republic, "the delegation of the Government . . . to a small number of citizens elected by the rest," who will "refine and enlarge the public views, by passing them through the medium of a chosen body of citizens, whose wisdom may best discern the true interest of their country, and whose patriotism and love of justice, will be least likely to sacrifice it to temporary or partial considerations."

In addition to representative mixed government, Madison found in federalism protection against the excesses of people's factional interests and passions. The size of the new republic, Madison argues, comprising as it does thirteen states each with its own government, will lessen the

---

52. Madison 10, 43–44.

ill effects of faction. Federalism will allow local concerns and competing interests to work themselves out in the state governments, but those factional interests will be unable to enlist the complicity of the whole republic because the federal government comprises legislators from all thirteen states, all of whom represent different and conflicting interests. Thus there will be a "greater security afforded by a greater variety of parties, against the event of any one party being able to outnumber and oppress the rest," and "greater obstacles opposed to the concert and accomplishment of the secret wishes of an unjust and interested majority." Any passionate interest pursued by demagogues or stoked by religious disputes, "will be unable to spread a general conflagration through the other states," and "the variety of sects dispersed over the entire face of it [the nation] must secure the national Councils against any danger from that source."[53] Just as the free market melds the private and clashing economic interests of countless individuals into prosperity for the whole, so the Constitution balances the selfish "passions and interests" of individuals, "factions," and states in order to protect freedom and political order for all.

The Constitutional Checks on Democratic Excess

The mixed government was designed to avoid the concentration of power in any branch that could threaten the freedom of the whole. Given a universally depraved human nature, an individual of notable talents and achievements, or an elite defined by wisdom, birth, or blood, was as much to be feared as the masses if it possessed too much power. Thus some arguments for an appointed rather than an elected Senate saw it as a way to balance one self-interested economic faction against another. New Yorker Gouverneur Morris, accepting the classical denigration of the fickle masses, argued for a state-appointed Senate "to check the precipitation, changeableness, and excesses of the first branch," something to expect given the recent disorder of the state legislatures, in which were seen "in every department excesses [against] personal lib-

---

53. Madison 10, 46–48; cf. Hamilton 60, 309.

erty private property & personal safety." But rather than check those potential excesses with an elite superior by virtue of wisdom, family, and knowledge, Morris focused on the clashing private interests of the poor and the rich, those of "great personal property" and the "aristocratic spirit." And what is the "interest" of the rich? "The Rich will strive to establish their dominion & enslave the rest. They always did. They always will. The proper security [against] them is to form them into a separate interest. The two forces will then countroul [sic] each other. . . . By thus combining & setting apart, the aristocratic interest, the popular interest will be combined [against] it. There will be a mutual check and mutual security."[54] Morris was not willing to rely on a Platonic natural aristocracy based on virtue and wisdom, preferring instead to accept that all men first and foremost pursue their material interests and flatter their own pride.

Yet distrust of the people predominates in the thinking of the founders, and it accounts for many constitutional structures designed to minimize the collective power of the masses, particularly the Supreme Court, the Senate, and the presidential electors, our Electoral College.

A Supreme Court of judges appointed for life by the president and confirmed by the Senate was necessary for defending against what James Madison called "Legislative encroachments" on the powers of the less democratic judiciary and the executive. The recent history of the state legislatures had shown "a powerful tendency in the legislature to absorb all power into its vortex. This was the real source of danger to the American Constitutions; & suggested the necessity of giving every defensive authority to the other departments that was consistent with republican principles." Gouverneur Morris, like Madison arguing unsuccessfully in support of an explicit rather than implicit constitutional provision for judicial review, evoked the antidemocratic fears of popular legislatures as necessary for blocking the legislative branch. When "bad laws" are legislated, "a strong check will be necessary." Such "bad laws" for Morris comprised the usual antidemocratic suspects: "Emissions of paper money, largesses [sic] to the people—a remission of debts and similar

---

54. Farrand, vol. 1, 512–13.

measures, will at sometimes [sic] be popular." Also the "interests of the legislators themselves" will lead to laws dangerous for the nation as a whole. Nor can the people be relied on to act as a sufficient check. "It might be thought that the people will not be deluded and misled in the latter case. But experience teaches another lesson." That "experience" no doubt was the popular disorders like the Fort Wilson Riot and Shays' Rebellion.[55]

The same concern with the excesses of the masses lay behind the structure of the Senate. While discussing what the number of senators from each state should be, Edmund Randolph deferred from giving a number, but commented "that they ought to be less than the House of Commons [Representatives]," and he "was for offering such a check as to keep up the balance, and to restrain, if possible, the fury of democracy."[56] Most revealing is the appointment of senators by state legislatures instead of being voted into office by the people, a practice in use until 1913, when the Seventeenth Amendment established the popular election of senators. At the convention John Dickinson of Delaware wanted senators appointed by the states "because he wished the Senate to consist of the most distinguished characters, distinguished for their rank in life and their weight of property, and bearing as strong a likeness to the British House of Lords as possible; and he thought such characters more likely to be selected by the State Legislatures than in any other mode." Later in the debate, Dickinson argued for a Senate of more than two hundred members whose "wealth, family, or Talents may hold them up to the State Legislatures as fit characters for the Senate." Thus "by combining the families and wealth of the aristocracy, you establish a balance that will check the Democracy."[57]

In the debates over the Senate during the convention, the antidemocratic tradition laced the arguments of many framers. Alexander Hamilton on June 18 highlighted the people's turbulence and lack of wisdom, and the need for a balancing legislative branch even more powerful than

---

55. Farrand, vol. 1, 74, 76.
56. Farrand, vol. 1, 58.
57. Farrand, vol. 1, 150, 158.

the Senate ultimately codified in the Constitution. Hamilton first invoked the principle of power's universal ability to corrupt, and hence the need for a balance of power: "Give all power to the many, they will oppress the few. Give all power to the few they will oppress the many. Both therefore ought to have power, that each may defend itself [against] the other." Moreover, like the ancient critics of democracy, Hamilton sees civil discord as arising out of the natural division of "the few and the many. The first are the rich and the well born, the other the mass of the people."

Given the excesses of democracy in the previous decade, which seemingly confirmed this natural class warfare, Hamilton is concerned with a legislative branch strong enough to resist the "amazing violence & turbulence of the democratic spirit. When a great object of Govt. is pursued, which seizes the popular passions, they spread like wild fire, and become irresistible. He appealed to the gentleman from the N. England States whether experience had not there verified the remark," a clear reference to Shays' Rebellion. Thus Hamilton wanted senators to hold office for life, unless disqualified by bad behavior.[58] "Only a senate rendered splendid and independent," historian Paul Rahe summarizes Hamilton's remarks and private notes, "in this fashion 'would induce the sacrifice of private affairs which an acceptance of public trust would require, so as to ensure the services of the best Citizens.'" Only such a body would be "capable of resisting the popular current," "check the imprudence of democracy" and "their turbulent and uncontrouling [sic] disposition," and "form a permanent barrier [against] every pernicious innovation."[59]

Eight days later James Madison similarly argued for the Senate and its structure on the basis of its presumed superiority in wisdom, judgment, and prudence over the more numerous and less exclusive House. Since the people "as well as a numerous body of Representatives, were liable to err also, from fickleness and passion . . . a necessary fence [against] this danger would be to select a portion of enlightened citizens, whose limited number, and firmness might seasonably impose [against] impetuous

---

58. Farrand, vol. 1, 299, 288–89, 299; cf. 310.
59. *Republics Ancient and Modern*, vol. 3, 115.

councils." Moreover, such a body would also protect against the dangers of factions, particularly the threat to minority rights, and the "leveling spirit," "symptoms" of which, Madison notes, referring no doubt to Shays' Rebellion, "have sufficiently appeared in a certain quarters to give notice of the future danger. How is the danger in all cases of interested co-alitions [sic] to oppress the minority to be guarded [against]? Among other means by the establishment of a body in the Govt. sufficiently respectable for its wisdom & virtue, to aid on such emergencies, the preponderance of justice by throwing its weight into that scale."[60]

In their more public arguments for the Senate, the *Federalist* writers emphasized its role in protecting federalism by giving the states an internal counterweight to the federal government. Answering the Antifederalist's concern that state sovereignty would be swallowed up by the federal government, for example, Madison lists the appointment by the state legislatures of senators and members of the Electoral College, and then concludes, "Thus each of the principal branches of the federal Government will owe its existence more or less to the favor of the State Governments, and must consequently feel a dependence, which is much more likely to beget a disposition too obsequious, than too overbearing toward them."[61] Yet the defense of the Senate still relied on the notion that the mass of people required a superior body of the more respectable and wise to check their excesses.

Alexander Hamilton argued for the likely greater efficiency of the federal government partly because senators would be chosen by state legislatures, "select bodies of men." Thus "there is reason to expect that this branch will be generally composed with peculiar care and judgment; That these circumstances promise greater knowledge and more extensive information in the national councils: And that they will be less apt to be tainted by the spirit of faction, and more out of the reach of those occasional ill humors or temporary prejudices and propensities, which . . . beget injustice and oppression of a part of the community, and engender schemes, which though they gratify a momentary

---

60. Farrand, vol. 1, 422–23; cf. 427–28, 430–31.
61. Madison 45, 237.

inclination or desire, terminate in general distress, dissatisfaction and disgust."[62] These remarks would not be out of place in Plato's argument for a government of elite "Guardians" in the *Republic*.

Madison is subtler, highlighting the smaller number of senators and their longer tenure as the mechanisms that will avoid the turbulence of larger democratic assemblies, which have a propensity "to yield to the impulse of sudden and violent passions, and to be seduced by factious leaders, into intemperate and pernicious resolutions." These traditional tropes of the antidemocratic tradition are joined to another, the "want of due acquaintance with the objects and principles of legislation. It is not possible that an assembly of men called for the most part from pursuits of a private nature, continued in appointment for a short time, and led by no permanent motive to devote the intervals of public occupation to a study of the laws, the affairs and the comprehensive interests of their country, should, if left wholly to themselves, escape a variety of important errors in the exercise of their legislative trust."[63]

In his next essay, Madison again diplomatically argues that given the volatility and passion of the many, "such an institution may be sometimes necessary, as a defense to the people against their own temporary errors and delusions," for "there are particular moments in public affairs, when the people stimulated by some irregular passion, or some illicit advantage, or misled by the artful misrepresentations of interested men, may call for measures which they themselves will afterwards be the most ready to lament and condemn. In these critical moments, how salutary will be the interference of some temperate and respectable body of citizens, in order to check the misguided career, and to suspend the blow meditated by the people against themselves, until reason, justice and truth, can regain their authority over the public mind?" Revealing the classical influences on his antidemocratic sentiments, Madison recalls the ancient Athenians and the "tyranny of their own passions" as the historic exemplar supporting his argument.[64]

---

62. Hamilton 27, 136–37.
63. Madison 62, 321.
64. Madison 63, 325–26.

Like the Senate, the executive branch of the new government was also protected from the turbulent masses by the mechanism of selecting the president by electors chosen by the states. In the debate over selecting the chief magistrate, some delegates did argue for popular election. Madison, for example, worried that the executive and the federal government would be too subordinate to the state governments. Some delegates proposed selection by the national legislature, but that ran the danger of weakening the authority of the executive by subordinating it to Congress, and the creation of cabals and intrigues between the two branches. In the end, however, popular election was rejected for the most part based on distrust of the people.

Elbridge Gerry, pondering these various alternatives, opposed out of hand popular election, doubting "that the people ought to act directly even in [the] choice of [state] electors, being too little informed of personal characters in large districts, and liable to deception."[65] The last objection, which assumed that the mass of people were incapable of transcending their parochial local interests, was repeated by Gouverneur Morris, who said "it would be as unnatural to refer the choice of a proper character for chief Magistrate to the people, as it would, to refer a trial of colours to a blind man," for "the extent of the Country renders it impossible that the people can have the requisite capacity to judge of the respective pretensions of the Candidates."[66] Gerry reprised his concerns a few days later, opposing popular election because "the people are uninformed, and would be misled by a few designing men." And reflecting the old antidemocratic charge that the people are fickle and use their power of electoral accountability to punish those who ignore or compromise their interests, he added, "The popular mode of electing the chief Magistrate would certainly be worst of all. If he should be so elected & if he should do his duty, he will be turned out for it."[67]

The method codified in the Constitution for choosing the president is selection by electors chosen by the state legislatures. The Constitu-

---

65. Farrand, vol. 1, 80.
66. Farrand, vol. 2, 31.
67. Farrand, vol. 2, 57.

tion leaves it up to the states to decide how presidential electors are selected. In the first presidential election of 1788, five state legislatures appointed the electors, while four others did so through popular votes using varying procedures. In a reflection of the increasing democratic sentiment discussed below, by 1830 every state except South Carolina chose electors by popular election.

The purpose of what we call the Electoral College, apart from being another way to strengthen state sovereignty, was to provide an additional layer of defense against the uninformed, self-interested, turbulent masses. As John Jay argued in *The Federalist*, selection by appointed electors has "vastly the advantage of elections by the people in their collective capacity, where the activity of party zeal taking advantage of the supineness, the ignorance, and the hopes and fears of the unwary and interested, often places men in office by the votes of a small proportion of the electors." Jay continues, since the "select assemblies" for choosing the president "will in general be composed of the most enlightened and respectable citizens, there is reason to presume that their attention and their votes will be directed to those men only who have become the most distinguished by their abilities and virtue, and in whom the people perceive just grounds for their confidence."[68] Alexander Hamilton makes a similar argument. Rather than trusting the people directly to choose the president, the framers found it "desirable, that the immediate election should be made by men most capable of analyzing the qualities adapted to the station, and acting under circumstances favorable to deliberation and to a judicious combination of all the reasons and inducements" proper for making a choice. Such "circumstances" need, moreover, "as little opportunity as possible to tumult and disorder." Hence allowing the people to choose, whether directly or indirectly, the several electors, "will be much less apt to convulse the community, with any extraordinary or violent movements" than the people choosing directly the President.[69]

Implicit in all these arguments is the assumption that the mass of people cannot be trusted, and that their collective sovereignty must be

---

68. Jay 64, 331.
69. Hamilton 68, 352.

indirectly exercised and tempered through "successive filtrations," as Madison termed it during the debates, a selection of men superior because of their virtues, knowledge, status, or experience.[70] In that way, as Madison writes in *The Federalist* 10, the system will "refine and enlarge the public views, by passing them through the medium of a chosen body of citizens, whose wisdom may best discern the true interest of their country, and whose patriotism and love of justice, will be least likely to sacrifice it to temporary or partial considerations."[71] These "filters" would ensure that the excesses of the turbulent, volatile masses would not be given the scope to act on their selfish passions and interests.

Democratizing the Franchise

The ratification of the Constitution did not end the strong democratic sentiment that had animated the Antifederalists and many other Americans. Critics of the new order attacked it explicitly in terms of its antidemocratic institutions, which they believed in time would empower the wealthy at the expense of the rest. Even for some of the framers, the Constitution seemed designed to empower an elite.

In his notes on the Constitution later published as a pamphlet, Virginia's George Mason, who did not sign the final draft of the Constitution, wrote of the Senate that "their power in the appointment of ambassadors and all public officers, in making treaties, and in trying all impeachments, their influence upon and connection with the supreme Executive from these causes, their duration of office and their being a constantly existing body, almost continually sitting, joined with their being one complete branch of the legislature, will destroy any balance in the government, and enable them to accomplish what ursurpations [sic] they please upon the rights and liberties of the people." He objected as well to the Supreme Court, which he feared would "absorb and destroy the judiciaries of the several States; thereby rendering law as tedious, intricate, and expensive, justice as attainable, by a great part of the com-

---

70. Farrand, vol. 1, 50.
71. Madison 10, 47.

munity, as in England, and enabling the rich to oppress and ruin the poor." The president, unchecked by an independent Council of State, will be "unsupported by proper information and advice, and will generally be directed by minions and favorites; or he will become a tool of the Senate." Ultimately, Mason concludes, "This government will set out [commence] a moderate aristocracy: it is at present impossible to foresee whether it will, in its operation, produce a monarchy, or a corrupt, tyrannical [oppressive] aristocracy."[72]

During the state ratifying conventions that started in December 1787, similar concerns were voiced in the debates and in the press about the oligarchical, antidemocratic dimensions of the Constitution. The Antifederalist commentator "Cincinnatus," Arthur Lee, in November 1787 darkly warned in the *New York Journal* that the constitutional "project is to burthen them [the people] with enormous taxes, in order to raise and maintain armies, for the purposes of ambition and arbitrary power—that this power is to be vested in an aristocratic senate, who will either be themselves the tyrants, or the support of tyranny, in a president, who will know how to manage them, so as to make that body at once the instrument and the shield of his absolute authority."[73] The following February, the like-minded "Agrarius" predicted in Philadelphia's *The Independent Gazetteer,* "The substantial yeomanry of America, the most valuable part of the community, will give place to lawyers and statesmen, who, in time, will engross all property, and thus the inhabitants of America will consist of two classes, the very rich and the very poor." Maryland's Samuel Chase in June of 1788 wrote to a correspondent, "I consider the Constitution as radically defective in this essential: the bulk of the people can have nothing to say to it. The government is *not* a government of the people. It is *not* a government of representation."[74] During the Virginia convention the same month, Patrick Henry complained, "The stile of the Government (we the people) was intro-

---

72. Farrand, vol. 2, 638, 640. Brackets indicate additions or changes Mason made before printing.
73. *The Debate on the Constitution*, vol. 1, 114.
74. In Main, *The Antifederalists*, 174, 175.

duced perhaps to recommend it to the people at large, to those citizens who are to be leveled and degraded to the lowest degree; who are likened to a *herd;* and who by the operation of this *blessed* system are to be transformed from respectable citizens, to abject, dependent subjects or slaves."[75]

This discontent persisted after ratification. During Washington's second term, numerous "Democratic-Republican" societies began to spring up, with as many as fifty by 1800, after which the success of Thomas Jefferson's Republican party made them superfluous. Inspired by the French Revolution, and angered by Federalist policies that seemingly catered to the rich and well connected, their members combined a distrust of concentrated power and its tendency to tyranny and corruption, with a populist disdain for "all the faulty finery brilliant scenes and expensive Trappings of Royal Government," as one Pennsylvanian put it.[76] They scorned as well the antidemocratic "monkish and dishonorable doctrine which teaches the original depravity of mankind," as New York lawyer Tunis Wortman orated in 1796, and that justified the "filters" between the people and the exercise of their sovereignty.[77] In 1800, Wortman wrote of arch-Federalist John Adams, "Mr. Adams is the advocate of privileged orders and distinctions in society, he would willingly engraft the armorial trappings and insignia of aristocracy upon the simple majesty of republican institutions. Mr. Adams would destroy the essential nature and character of a republic; his principles would wrest the government from the hands of the people, and vest its dominion and prerogatives in the distinguished and 'well born few.'"[78] And appealing to the fear of corruption wrought by elites with power, the German Republican Society in 1794 asserted that their organization's aim was "to guard against those encroachments, which all Governments

---

75. *The Debate on the Constitution*, vol. 2, 634.

76. Sean Wilentz, *The Rise of American Democracy* (New York, 2005), 41, 809 n. 2.

77. In *The Democratic-Republican Societies*, ed. Philip S. Foner (Westport, CT, 1976), 22.

78. "A Solemn Address to Christians and Patriots," http://oll.libertyfund.org /?option=com_staticxt&staticfile=show.php%3Ftitle=817&chapter=69460& layout=html&Itemid=27.

endeavor to make upon the People's rights. The despotism which Man too generally inclines to exercise, makes caution necessary—His disposition to avail himself of opportunities for domination, ought to beget an attention, that more should not be committed to him than necessity extorts."[79] George Cabot of Boston summarized this widespread democratic sentiment in 1801: "The spirit of our country is doubtless more democratic than the *form* of our government."[80]

Beginning with the Revolution, this discontent with the perceived democracy deficit was expressed most directly in state movements to broaden the franchise by loosening voting requirements. The American colonies had taken from England the "stakeholder" principle underlying voting rights. "Freeholders," free males of legal age who owned property, were given the right to vote because they were considered more economically self-sufficient and stable, and hence their electoral choices more independent and responsible than those of men of "so mean a situation as to be esteemed to have no will of their own," as the influential jurist William Blackstone wrote. Such people would be dependent on the more powerful and wealthy, and hence more likely to trade their votes for private advantage, thus corrupting the political process.[81] And a wider suffrage would multiply those conflicting factions and parties that historically had been the bane of republics, a belief based on the assumption documented above that most men use political power to further their own passions, beliefs, and interests.

Given these beliefs, throughout the colonies the ownership of property worth some minimum value was a prerequisite for voting, and higher qualifications were necessary for holding office. The qualifying amount for voting varied. In Rhode Island, land worth forty pounds or forty shillings in annual rental value qualified for the franchise; in New Hampshire the rate was fifty pounds. Most colonies calculated the value in acres, such as in Virginia, where a hundred acres of unimproved land, or twenty-five of improved were required to vote. Others used the value

---

79. In Foner, 73.
80. In Williamson, *American Suffrage*, 174.
81. In Williamson, 11.

of annual income, as in Massachusetts, which put the rate at forty shillings. The other alternatives to a freehold qualification were possession of property other than land rated at a minimum value, or payment of taxes. As Chilton Williamson writes, "colonial suffrage legislation . . . was designed to confine the vote to desirable elements of the population. It was drafted in the conviction that efficiency, honesty, and harmony in government rested, in the last analysis, upon a salutary degree of homogeneity of interests, opinions, and fundamental loyalties—religious, ethnic, and class." Thus limiting the vote to free male property owners would minimize "undue disparities of interest, opinion, and loyalty among electors" that led to destructive factionalism.[82]

The war against England—with its rhetoric of freedom, equality, popular sovereignty, and the right to participate in government—stoked demands for the liberalization of suffrage requirements. Too many Americans who had fought and struggled in the war were shut out from political participation. Despite widespread availability of land, Forrest McDonald writes, "only about one American in six was eligible to participate in the political process, and far fewer were eligible to hold public office."[83] Indeed, only 1.5 percent of Americans had voted to ratify the Constitution.[84] Even still, fewer than half the new states made significant reforms to their voting requirements, most notable Pennsylvania and North Carolina, which allowed all taxpayers to vote. Yet even modest efforts to widen the franchise elicited the traditional antidemocratic worries over the malign effects of unchecked popular power.

During the Constitutional Convention, for example, a debate arose over qualifications for those electing the House of Representatives. The draft of the article in the Constitution concerning electors set the qualifications as the same "as those of the electors in the several States, of the most numerous branch of their own legislatures." In most states this "branch" had the lowest qualifications, including many that did not require ownership of property. Gouverneur Morris made a motion

---

82. Williamson, 19.
83. *Novus Ordo Seclorum*, 162.
84. McDougall, *Freedom Just around the Corner*, 308.

to strike out the language regarding the states, "that some other provision might be substituted which wd. restrain the right of the suffrage to freeholders."[85]

During the debate that followed, the old antidemocratic prejudices were aired to support the "stakeholder" view of voting rights that had predominated before the Revolution. Delaware's John Dickinson, arguing for restricting the franchise to freeholders, called them "the best guardians of liberty," and the "restriction of the right [to vote] to them as a necessary defence [sic] [against] the dangerous influence of those multitudes without property & without principle, with which our Country like all others, will in time abound." Morris evoked the argument that those without property, being dependent on the more powerful, will be vulnerable to the ambitious rich: "Give the votes to people who have no property, and they will sell them to the rich who will be able to buy them." Given the growth of "mechanics & manufacturers, who will receive their bread from their employers," these economically dependent workers will not "be the impregnable barrier [against] aristocracy" necessary for protecting freedom against the dominance of an elite. Sounding like Socrates or Plato, Morris snorted, "The ignorant & the dependent can be little trusted with the public interest." John Francis Mercer of Maryland, who did not sign the final draft of the Constitution, likewise sounded the antidemocratic theme: "The people can not know & judge of the characters of the candidates. The worse possible choice will be made."[86]

Morris's motion failed, the opposition to it reflecting pragmatic concerns that restricting the vote to freeholders would "depress the virtue & public spirit of our common people" who had fought in the war, as Benjamin Franklin argued, and "would create division among the people & make enemies of all those who should be excluded," according to John Rutledge, whose home state of South Carolina had one of the more liberal suffrage requirements.[87]

---

85. Farrand, vol. 2, 201.
86. Farrand, vol. 2, 202–3, 205.
87. Farrand, vol. 2, 204–5.

As soon became clear in the following years, the antidemocratic traditionalists like Morris, Mercer, and Dickinson were swimming against the populist tide. In the next decades after ratification, reforms in most states either eliminated the freehold requirement, as in Vermont, Maryland, and South Carolina, while in the remaining states, except Connecticut and Massachusetts, the right to vote was based "upon a taxpaying qualification which amounted to universal manhood suffrage wherever all adult males were subject to the payment of a poll tax," as Chilton Williamson writes. Pennsylvania architect Benjamin H. Latrobe, one of the designers of the Capitol in Washington, articulated this trend in 1806: "After the adoption of the Federal Constitution, the extension of the right of suffrage in the States to a majority of all the adult male citizens, planted a germ which had [sic] gradually evolved and has spread actual and practical democracy and political equality over the whole union."[88] By the mid-nineteenth century the right to vote without a property qualification—though other restrictions would remain—was universally accepted, and it became a campaign issue popular with all parties.

Democratizing the Republic

As early as 1792 the division between democrats and antidemocrats visible in the framing of the Constitution and the debates over suffrage qualifications had created two dominant factions that would soon coalesce into political parties. The "Federalists"—"Anti-republicans" or "Monocrats" to their rivals—endorsed the traditional distrust of the people that lay behind much of the structure of the Constitution. "Republicans" considered the Constitution to be compatible with popular self-rule and broader participation in government.[89] In 1792, one of the driving forces behind the Republicans, James Madison, polemically defined the two parties in these terms:

---

88. In Williamson, 209.
89. By Jackson's presidency Republicans had divided into National Republicans and Democratic Republicans, the latter soon to become Democrats. The modern Republican Party was created in 1854.

One of the divisions consists of those, who from particular interest, from natural temper, or from the habits of life, are more partial to the opulent than to the other classes of society; and having debauched themselves into a persuasion that mankind are incapable of governing themselves, it follows with them, of course, that government can be carried on only by the pageantry of rank, the influence of money and emoluments, and the terror of military force. Men of those sentiments must naturally wish to point the measures of government less to the interest of the many than of a few, and less to the reason of the many than to their weaknesses; hoping perhaps in proportion to the ardor of their zeal, that by giving such a turn to the administration, the government itself may by degrees be narrowed into fewer hands, and approximated to an hereditary form.

The other division consists of those who believing in the doctrine that mankind are capable of governing themselves, and hating hereditary power as an insult to the reason and an outrage to the rights of man, are naturally offended at every public measure that does not appeal to the understanding and to the general interest of the community, or that is not strictly conformable to the principles, and conducive to the preservation of republican government.[90]

The Federalists responded with the traditional antidemocratic tropes about the turbulent masses and the dangers of tyranny that always follow the surrender of power to the passionate and self-interested people.

For example, commenting on the Kentucky Democratic Society in 1794, "Xantippe" dismissed them as "that horrible sink of treason,— that hateful synagogue of anarchy,—that odious conclave of tumult . . . that hellish school of rebellion and opposition to all regular and well-balanced authority." A year later editor William Cobbett socratically scorned them as "butchers, tinkers, broken hucksters, and trans-Atlantic traitors."[91] The Whiskey Rebellion of 1794, a protest among Western Pennsylvanians against a tax on whiskey, for many antidemocrats confirmed their fears of violent revolution erupting among the volatile

90. *The National Gazette*, September 26, 1792, http://oll.libertyfund.org/?option
   =com_staticxt&staticfile=show.php%3Ftitle=1941&chapter=124404&
   layout=html&Itemid=27.
91. Foner, *The Democratic-Republican Societies*, 7, 27.

common people and stirred up by the Democratic-Republican societies. Indeed, Alexander Hamilton and President Washington partly blamed the Democratic-Republican societies for the rebellion.

Like the Fort Wilson Riot and Shays' Rebellion, the Whiskey Rebellion provoked traditional antidemocratic attacks. In 1803, Federalist newspapers reprinted remarks from journalist and editor Joseph Dennie, who wrote, "A democracy is scarcely tolerable at any period of national history. Its omens are always sinister, and its powers are unpropitious. It is on trial here, and the issue will be civil war, desolation, and anarchy. No wise man but discerns its imperfections, no good man but shudders at its miseries, no honest man but proclaims its fraud, and no brave man but draws his swords against its force."[92] Dennie was charged (later acquitted) with seditious libel for this attack on democracy. A few years later in 1805, Massachusetts Congressman Fisher Ames reprised in a private letter the ancient link of extreme democracy and military despotism: "A democracy cannot last. Its nature ordains that its next change shall be into a military despotism. . . . The reason is that the tyranny of what is called the people, and that by the sword, both operate alike to debase and corrupt, till there are neither men left with the spirit to desire liberty, nor morals with the power to sustain justice."[93] At the end of his life in 1808, Ames lamented that only five hundred Federalists "allow themselves to view the progress of licentiousness as so speedy, so sure, and so fatal as the deplorable experience of our country shows that it is, and the evidence of history and the constitution of human nature demonstrate that it must be."[94]

Ames's tone of resignation calls to mind the Old Oligarch's more caustic comments on the triumphant Athenian democracy. After Ames's death in 1808, the private letter quoted from above was published as an essay, "The Dangers of American Liberty." In it Ames fires a farewell

---

92. In Henry Adams, *History of the United States of America during the Administrations of Jefferson and Madison*, abr. and ed. Ernest Samuels (Chicago and London, 1967), 65.
93. "The Dangers of American Liberty," *The Works of Fisher Ames*, vol. 2, ed. Seth Ames (1854; Boston, 1971), 382.
94. Adams, 67.

salvo in defense of the antidemocratic tradition that had been so influential for the framers. Like that tradition, Ames believed extreme democracy must degenerate into tyranny: democracy, what Ames calls "licentiousness," will "prove, as it has ever proved, fatal to liberty," for "of all despotisms a democracy, though the least durable, is the most violent." The "clamors" of faction and party, moreover, with their pursuits of private passions and interests, make it impossible to convince anyone that "our democratic liberty is utterly untenable; that we are devoted to the successive struggles of factions, who will rule by turns, the worst of whom will rule last, and triumph by the sword," for it has never happened "that a democracy has been kept out of the control of the fiercest and most turbulent spirits in the society; they will breathe into it all their own fury, and make it subservient to the worst designs of the worst men."[95]

Ames goes on to catalogue the other traditional charges against democracy. The old fears of the turbulent, ignorant masses becoming prey to ambitious demagogues are also invoked by Ames: "The more free the citizens, the bolder and more profligate will be their demagogues, the more numerous and eccentric the popular errors, and the more vehement and pertinacious the passions that defend them." The radical egalitarianism mocked by Plato and Aristotle is part of Ames's indictment as well. "In a democracy, the elevation of an equal convinces many, if not all, that the height to which he is raised is not inaccessible. Ambition wakes from its long sleep in every soul . . . to turn its tortures into weapons against the public order." The use of political power to forgive debts and redistribute property, one of the oldest charges in the indictment of democracy, appears in Ames's warning that, "as property is the object of the great mass of every faction, the rules that keep it sacred will be annulled, or so far shaken, as to bring enough of it within the grasp of the dominant party to reward their partisans with booty." The result of such "extreme" democracy will be, as predicted by Polybius, Plato, and Aristotle, tyranny and the destruction of freedom, a particular danger in America, where the "low vulgar" are "so much less man-

---

95. In *The Works of Fisher Ames*, 346–47, 356.

ageable by their demagogues," and so "we are to expect that our affairs will be long guided by courting the mob, before they are violently changed by employing them."[96] Writing nearly a century later, when Ames's dark prophecies had seemingly been proven wrong, Henry Adams would attribute them to the outsized influence of the French Revolution's gruesome Reign of Terror, fear of which became for Ames a "morbid illusion." So completely had American democracy prevailed over the long antidemocratic tradition, that an eloquent expression of it could be dismissed as a form of neurosis.[97]

As in the debate over suffrage, the Republicans were more closely in tune with the growing democratic momentum of the country than were Federalists like Ames. In 1800 the two parties were as yet evenly balanced: Republican Thomas Jefferson barely won the presidency with the help of the machinations of Federalists more frightened of the opportunist Aaron Burr than of the "Jacobin" author of the Declaration of Independence. In his inaugural speech, however, Jefferson, though conciliatory, evoked the democratic ideals that would prevail in the coming decades. He seconded the Periclean democratic creed that the people, whatever their birth or wealth, are political equals, deserving of a "due sense of our equal right to the use of our own faculties, to the acquisitions of our own industry, to honor and confidence from our fellow-citizens, resulting not from birth, but from our actions and their sense of them." Against a government of concentrated power and a corrupted elite, Jefferson extolled "a wise and frugal Government, which shall restrain men from injuring one another, shall leave them otherwise free to regulate their own pursuits of industry and improvement, and shall not take from the mouth of labor the bread it has earned." And among his "general principles" of governing Jefferson included the democratic boons of "Equal and exact justice to all men, of whatever state or persuasion, religious or political," "a jealous care of the right

---

96. *The Works of Fisher Ames*, 382, 359–60, 368, 399.
97. Adams, *History of the United States of America During the Administrations of Jefferson and Madison*, 65.

of election by the people," and "absolute acquiescence in the decisions of the majority, the vital principle of republics."[98]

Jefferson's victory began an eventual Republican political domination—one soon riven, to be sure, by its own division between moderates and radicals, and by sectional conflicts over slavery— that culminated in the two terms of Andrew Jackson (1829–37), and that confirmed Jefferson's prediction early in his first term that he would "sink federalism into an abyss from which there shall be no resurrection for it."[99] During that period the understanding of "Republicanism" as protection against the dangers of democratic excess had changed into one that accepted a more democratic exercise of self-rule among the masses. The denigration of the people that was second nature to many of the political philosophers of the founding period was now a political liability, an opinion to keep to one's self for those who were politically ambitious.

One reason the Republicans flourished is that they spoke to the growing numbers of ambitious and enterprising common people who were being given the opportunity to improve their lot by an expanding economy and the abundance of land in the frontier. The enemies of this opportunity were the "closed elites," as Walter McDougall calls them. Their policies concentrated political power and wealth, and their gloomy Federalist philosophy justified this privilege with antidemocratic prejudices about a fallen human nature that made the ignorant, turbulent masses unfit to rule, and with scolding sermons denouncing the corrupting influences of wealth and development. Republican literature, McDougall writes, instead celebrated the abilities of average people that allowed them to take advantage of economic opportunity and improve their lives. As such, Republican tracts did not condemn markets, but only "markets people could not *participate* in for lack of sufficient money or status, or just for living too far afield. No wonder states' right advocates, back-country people, urban mechanics and storekeepers, social

---

98. Thomas Jefferson's First Inaugural Address, http://avalon.law.yale.edu/19th
    _century/jefinau1.asp.
99. In Wilentz, 97.

climbers, and immigrants voted Republican. So did pioneers, planters, and frontier lawyers who were by no means opposed to getting rich quick, but rejected the idea that that such aspirations were corrupt (Hamilton) or corrupting (Adams) *so long* as they were not restricted to exclusive elites." The Republicans, in short, preached "a society of equals in which everyone had a fair shot to get rich in an ever expanding economy."[100] The desire for more political participation and access to office was a natural corollary of this economic and social improvement. As historian Sean Wilentz writes of the explosion in political activity by ordinary people, "The filters on democracy created by the Framers were proving porous, while the suppression of democracy sought by the Federalists in the 1790s was thoroughly discredited."[101]

Given these improvements in the prospects of ordinary Americans, during those three decades between the first administration of Jefferson and the last of Jackson, the fear of a quasi-aristocratic elite—empowered by the federal government and vulnerable to the corruptions of concentrated power—came to trump the traditional anxiety over the "licentiousness" and "leveling spirit" of the fickle, ignorant, self-interested masses. The rhetoric of Andrew Jackson played upon this shift, now contrasting the rehabilitated common people with the federal government under a Federalist administration, which "is calculated to raise around the administration a moneyed aristocracy dangerous to the liberties of the country," as he wrote in 1824. This fear of federal corruption was seemingly confirmed in the presidential election of that same year, when Jackson received a plurality of votes but was denied office through the machinations of John Quincy Adams and Kentucky's Henry Clay after the election was thrown into the House of Representatives, of which Clay was a member. This unsavory election, as historian Robert Remini writes, "unleashed the democratic storm that had been building for years—if not decades—and radically changed the system of government in all its branches as well as between constituen-

---

100. McDougall, 364–66; emphases in original.
101. Wilentz, 139.

cies. Moreover, it provided the philosophic basis by which the American electorate viewed and interpreted government and its functions."[102]

Jackson's political philosophy was democratic far beyond the sensibilities of most of the founders. He understood popular sovereignty much more directly than did they, who filtered it through representation by those superior in virtue and wisdom, and who considered the Constitution and its delegation of power to be the final expression of the people's will, to be changed only by the difficult process of amendment. In contrast, to Jackson, "Our government is founded upon the intelligence of the people. . . . I have great confidence in the virtue of the great majority of the people."[103] As president, in 1835 he wrote, "The people are the government, administering it by their agents; they are the Government, the sovereign power," and "their will is absolute."[104]

As such, he looked with suspicion on the antidemocratic "filtering" institutions such as the Supreme Court, the Electoral College, and the Senate. In 1832, he vetoed legislation renewing the charter of the Bank of the United States, despite a Supreme Court ruling establishing its constitutionality. "Mere precedent," Jackson wrote in his veto, "is a dangerous source of authority, and should not be regarded as deciding questions of constitutional power except where the acquiescence of the people and the States can be considered as well as settled. . . . The authority of the Supreme Court must not, therefore, be permitted to control the Congress or the Executive when acting in their legislative capacities, but to have only such influence as the force of their reasoning may deserve."[105] Having lost the presidency in 1824 in the House of Representatives, Jackson was also understandably hostile to the Electoral College. "To the people," he said in his first annual message, "belongs the right of electing the Chief Magistrate; it was never designed that their choice should in any case be defeated, either by the interven-

---

102. In Robert V. Remini, *The Legacy of Andrew Jackson* (Baton Rouge and London, 1988), 12, 14.
103. In Remini, 38.
104. In Remini, 23–24.
105. James D. Richardson, ed., *A Compilation of the Messages and Papers of the Presidents* (New York, 1897), vol. 3, 1144–45.

tion of electoral colleges or by the agency confided, under certain contingencies, to the House of Representatives. Experience proves that in proportion as agents to execute the will of the people are multiplied there is danger of their wishes being frustrated. . . . So far, therefore, as the people can with convenience speak, it is safer for them to express their own will." He went on to call for a constitutional amendment to "remove all intermediate agency in the election" of the president to empower "the free operation of the public will" in order to achieve "a fair expression of the will of the majority."[106] As for the Senate, Remini writes, to Jackson it was "an elitist body of men committed to the principles of aristocracy and totally unrepresentative of the American people." The Republican newspaper the *Washington Globe* called for limiting to four years the terms of senators, and having the people directly elect them.[107]

Other democratic principles endorsed by Jackson included the "right to instruction," the doctrine, as stated in 1835 in a resolution by the New Jersey General Assembly, that "whereas in all representative government, the sovereignty of the People is an indisputable truth, they have the right and it is their duty, upon all proper occasions, to instruct their representatives in the duties which they require them to perform." Jackson agreed, posing as a political litmus test the questions whether supposed Republicans "subscribe to the republican rule that the people are the sovereign power, the officers their agents & representative, and they are bound to obey or resign."[108] Finally, Jackson supported the democratic principle of "rotation," limitations put on the tenure of government officials to preclude the creation of a permanent ruling elite prone to abusing their power for their own ends and thus endangering the freedom of the whole. Few men, Jackson said in his first annual address, "can for any great length of time enjoy office and power without being more or less under the influence of feelings unfavorable to the faithful discharge of their public duties" and, though themselves perhaps men of integrity, "are apt to acquire a habit of look-

---

106. Richardson, 3.1010–11.
107. Remini, 34.
108. Remini, 36.

ing with indifference upon the public interest and of tolerating conduct
from which an unpracticed man would revolt. . . . Corruption in some
and in others a perversion of correct feelings and principles divert government from its legitimate ends and make it an engine for the support
of the few at the expense of the many."[109] As Jackson wrote in his memo-
randum book, "It is rotation in office that will perpetuate our liberty."[110]
We see here an echo of the old Athenian suspicion of elite power evident
in the one-year terms and procedures of accountability discussed above.
Reversing the philosophy of the Federalists codified in the Constitution,
now elites were more to be feared than the masses.

Antidemocrats at Bay

After the Jackson era, US political sentiment had moved decidedly
toward democracy and the rehabilitation of the masses. In 1835, William
Henry Seward, a member of the Whig party (the new political party
that developed in Jackson's second term), acknowledged this political
reality. Gloomily predicting the victory in the next year's presidential
election of Martin Van Buren, Jackson's secretary of state, Seward wrote,
"It is utterly impossible, I am convinced, to defeat Van Buren. The people
are for him. Not so much for him as for the principle they suppose he
represents. That principle is Democracy. . . . It is with them, the poor
against the rich; and it is not to be disguised, that, since the last election,
the array of parties has very strongly taken that character."[111] Indeed, "By
1837," Remini writes, the "word *democracy* had largely supplanted the
term *republicanism* in national discourse."[112]

   Though the federal government was still defined by the antidemocratic structures of the Constitution, in the court of public sentiment
the people had won. At first antidemocrat Federalists continued to protest
what they considered the triumph of the tumultuous masses. Jackson's

---

109. Richardson, 3.1011–12.
110. Remini, 31.
111. In Wilentz, 482.
112. Remini, 8.

legendary first inaugural festivities, in which the White House was thrown open to ordinary people, seemingly confirmed to critics all their prejudices about the unruly masses. To Supreme Court Justice Joseph Story, "the reign of KING MOB seemed triumphant."[113] Outgoing president John Quincy Adams left town instead of attending the celebration. Anne Newport Royall, considered by some to be the first female professional journalist, noted in the White House soiled sofas and carpets, and Jackson supporters who made "disgraceful scenes in the parlors, in which even women got bloody noses." Only a bowl of punch was able "to lure the new 'democracy' out of the house." As Walter McDougall writes, "Wondrous it was, and to the genteel a nightmare. Washington, Franklin, Madison, Hamilton, Adams, and Jefferson had imagined the American experiment coming to all sorts of bad ends. They *never* imagined the Federal City overrun by frontiersmen who care nothing for history and loved only cheap land and credit, whiskey, tobacco, guns, fast women, fast horses, and Jesus."[114]

By the time the Civil War started in 1861, the antidemocrats had long been at bay, and those seeking public office, Alexis de Tocqueville wrote, "hide their heads, and if they wish to rise are forced to borrow their colors."[115] The rival party to Jacksonian democracy, the Whigs, "devised a contrasting democratic message that struck a deep nerve in the electorate that the Democrats [as Republicans came to be called under Jackson] did not even realize was there," Wilentz writes. Whig political success was due to exploiting Jacksonian democracy's "own democratic political terms that old-guard conservatives had abhorred. By decade's end, Whigs and Democrats alike could agree in principle with Jacksonian paeans to the people and majority rule."[116]

With the triumph of democracy and the political eclipse of antidemocratic ideology, it was left to Alexis de Tocqueville, American democracy's most astute analyst and influential publicist, to acknowledge

---

113. In Wilentz, 312.
114. McDougall, 497.
115. In Williamson, 260.
116. Wilentz, 517.

democracy's weaknesses and dangers in his influential *Democracy in America*. "I sought there [America] the image of democracy itself," he wrote in the introduction to Book 1 (1835), "with its inclinations, its character, its prejudices, and its passions, in order to learn what we have to fear or to hope from its progress." His comments on democratic government, while more temperate than those of Federalist critics, nonetheless reprise many of the charges against democracy that comprised the antidemocratic tradition of the Old Oligarch, Socrates, Aristophanes, Thucydides, Plato, Aristotle, and Polybius, and their epigones in Americans like John Adams, Gouverneur Morris, and Fisher Ames.[117]

For example, Tocqueville finds that the lack of learning and the poor discernment of character among the common people empower demagogues and mediocre leaders. In the United States, Tocqueville writes, "The ablest men . . . are rarely placed at the head of affairs; and it must be acknowledged that such has been the result in proportion as democracy has exceeded all its former limits." He links this phenomenon to the common people's inability to devote enough time to acquiring the intellectual skills and knowledge necessary for choosing able leaders: "it is always more or less difficult for them [the "mass of the citizens"] to discern the best means of attaining the end ["the welfare of the country"] which they sincerely desire." Judging character is difficult in any case, he continues in the Socratic vein, but "the people have neither the time nor the means for an investigation of this kind. Their conclusions are hastily formed from a superficial inspection of the more prominent features of a question. Hence it often happens that mountebanks of all sorts are able to please the people, while their truest friends frequently fail to gain their confidence."[118]

Consequently, the "difficulty that a democracy finds in conquering the passions and subduing the desires of the moment with a view to the future" fosters the short-term, self-interested political decisions that

---

117. *Democracy in America*, vol. 1, ed. Philip Bradley, rev. Frances Bowen (New York, 1994), 14.
118. *Democracy in America*, 200–1.

Socrates, Thucydides, and Plato decried in ancient Athens. And like the Athenians, demagogues play a role in this political dysfunction: "The people, surrounded by flatterers, find great difficulty in surmounting their inclinations; whenever they are required to undergo a privation or any inconvenience, even to attain an end sanctioned by their own rational conviction, they almost always refuse at first to comply." As a result, "an offensive law of which the majority should not see the immediate utility would either not be enacted or not be obeyed." He cites the absence of laws controlling the sale of alcohol as an example of a law "offensive" to the masses despite the public disorder caused by drunkenness. Indeed, so strict is the accountability of demagogues to the people, and "the power of the majority is so absolute and irresistible that one must give up one's rights as a citizen and almost abjure one's qualities as a man if one intends to stray from the track which it proscribes."[119]

Tocqueville also worries that the tendency of democracies to promote radical egalitarianism, which in turn fuels demands for redistribution of property, may arise in the United States given its unprecedented social equality. This radical egalitarianism he calls "a depraved taste for equality, which impels the weak to attempt to lower the powerful to their own level and reduces men to prefer equality in slavery to inequality with freedom." He links this demand for equality to "democratic institutions" that "strongly tend to promote the feeling of envy in the human heart. . . . Democratic institutions awaken and foster a passion for equality which they can never satisfy." Tax policy is one way to attempt such leveling: "As the great majority of those who create the laws have no taxable property, all the money that is spent for the community appears to be spent for their advantage, at no cost of their own; and those who have some little property readily find means of so regulating the taxes that they weigh upon the wealthy and profit the poor, although the rich cannot take the same advantage when they are in possession of the government. . . . In other words, the government of the democracy is the only one under which the power that votes the

---

119. *Democracy in America*, 230, 267.

taxes escapes the payment of them." Hence "the government makes great efforts to satisfy the wants of the lower classes, to open to them the road to power, and to diffuse knowledge and comfort among them. The poor are maintained, immense sums are annually devoted to public instruction, all services are remunerated, and the humblest agents are liberally paid."[120] In these comments we hear many of the antidemocratic indictments of popular rule that had become political poison in national politics.

US Democracy's Next Phase

Such sentiments, however, could not tarnish the good name of democracy. The challenge to popular rule came instead from the institution of slavery, which undermined the assumptions of equality and the distaste for hierarchy that drove much of the Democrats' success, and weakened the Federalist idea of state sovereignty. The old fear of moneyed, quasi-aristocratic elites vulnerable to corruption by power and to the tyranny that followed saw in the Southern plantation class a danger to the integrity of democratic freedom and equality.

In April 1859, Abraham Lincoln, in a letter declining an invitation to celebrate Thomas Jefferson's birthday in Boston, put his finger on the shift in Democratic principles wrought by slavery. "The Jefferson party," Lincoln wrote, "were formed upon their supposed superior devotion to the *personal* rights of men, holding the rights of *property* to be secondary only, and greatly inferior." The implication is that the Federalists, as the Antifederalists had argued, were the party of elite rule designed in part to protect private property against the tendency of the democratic masses to redistribute wealth and seek forgiveness of debts, while the Jeffersonian Republicans were the party devoted to personal freedom and political equality. But now the proslavery Democrats "hold the *liberty* of one man to be absolutely nothing, when in conflict with another man's right of *property*." The newly formed Repub-

---

120. *Democracy in America*, 53, 201, 214, 224.

licans, the true heirs of Jefferson, "are for both the *man* and the *dollar;* but in cases of conflict, the man *before* the dollar." The proslavery Democrats have as their object "the supplanting the principles of free government, and restoring those of classification, caste, and legitimacy. They would delight a convocation of crowned heads, plotting against the people. They are the van-guard [sic]—the miners, and sappers—of returning despotism. We must repulse them, or they will subjugate us." This despotism is inherent in the institution of slavery, which compromises democratic equality and freedom, for "he who would *be* no slave, must consent to *have* no slave. Those who deny freedom to others, deserve it not for themselves."[121]

Once again, as it did at the creation of the Jeffersonian Republican Party, the fear of elites corrupted by power was more cogent than the fear of the tumultuous masses that had dominated the Constitutional Convention. Once again, democracy had to be defended against the despotism of "classification" and "caste." But this time, a bloody civil war had to be fought to protect equality and freedom, the foundations of US democracy.

Yet in defending and expanding this democracy by abolishing slavery and enfranchising blacks, the Civil War birthed a federal government more powerful and more intrusive on the rights and sovereignty of the states. Historian Paul Rahe catalogues these innovations:

> [T]he administration of Abraham Lincoln . . . transformed the American government in a fashion that would have fully satisfied Alexander Hamilton. To win the war, they reestablished a national bank, issued a federal currency, provided for an expansion of the national debt, and passed an elaborate, emergency program of federal taxation, including a progressive income tax. In its early stages, moreover, they imposed a tariff aimed at encouraging industrialization, and they instituted a program designed to promote the long-term economic well-being of the

---

121. *The Collected Works of Abraham Lincoln*, ed. Roy P. Balser (New Brunswick, NJ, 1953), vol. 3, 375–76.

American people. . . . From this time on, the Union was a real and continuing presence in the lives of ordinary Americans.[122]

In time these developments and others, under the growing stresses of
industrialization, urbanization, and an increasingly complex economy,
would expand and evolve, stretching the constitutional limits on the
federal government, and laying the groundwork for the democratic despotism that the ancient political theorists posited as the inevitable cul-
mination of extreme democracy.

---

122. *Soft Despotism, Democracy's Drift* (New Haven, CT, 2009), 243–44.

CHAPTER THREE

Democracy and Leviathan

So when they [the rich] begin to hanker after office, and find that they cannot achieve it through their own efforts or on their merits, they begin to seduce and corrupt the people in every possible way, and thus ruin their estates. The result is that through their senseless craving for prominence they stimulate among the masses both an appetite for bribes and the habit of receiving them, and then the rule of democracy is transformed into government by violence and strong-arm methods. By this time the people have become accustomed to feed at the expense of others, and their prospects of winning a livelihood depend upon the property of their neighbours; then as soon as they find a leader who is sufficiently ambitious and daring, but is excluded from the honours of office because of his poverty, they introduce a regime based on violence.

—Polybius[1]

Mankind soon learn to make interested uses of every right and power which they possess, or may assume. The public money and public liberty, intended to be deposited with three branches of magistracy, but found inadvertently to be in the hands of one only, will soon be discovered to be the source of wealth and dominion to those who hold them; distinguished too by this tempting circumstance, that they are the instrument, as well as the object of acquisition. . . . They [magistrates] should look forward to a time, and that not a distant one, when corruption in this . . . will have seized the heads of government, and be spread by them through the body of the people; when they will purchase the voices of the people, and make them pay the price.

—Thomas Jefferson[2]

---

1. *Histories* 6.9, trans. Ian Scott-Kilvert (Harmondsworth, England, 1979), 309.
2. *Notes on the State of Virginia* (1782); in *Writings*, ed. Merrill D. Peterson (New York, 1984), 246.

In the antidemocratic tradition, the flaws of democracy inevitably lead to tyranny. Radical egalitarianism and excessive freedom—what the founding generation called a "leveling spirit" and "license"—corrupt the masses, leaving them vulnerable to ambitious men or elites who in exchange for their political support promise the masses gratification of their wants and desires. Forgiveness of debts and redistribution of property are the mechanisms by which despotic regimes finance the hedonism of the people. But such leaders must continue to gratify the people's desire for licentious freedom if they want to stay in power. "When a democracy which is thirsting for freedom," Plato writes, "has evil cupbearers presiding over the feast, and has drunk too deeply of the strong wine of freedom, then, unless her rulers are very amenable and give a plentiful draught, she calls them to account and punishes them." Moreover, the propertied class must be plundered of its wealth both to finance this politically narcotic hedonism and to enrich the tyrant: "Do not the leaders deprive the rich of their estates and distribute them among the people; at the same time taking care to reserve the larger part for themselves?"[3] The result is a feedback loop between the tyrants' lust for power and the people's desire for wealth transfers that eventually destroys political freedom.

Aristotle in the *Politics* makes a similar argument in his analysis of how democracies degenerate into tyranny, in this case by provoking a backlash from the propertied few. The weakness of the laws, which in "extreme democracy" are vulnerable to the fickle and changing moods of the turbulent people who make them, begets demagogues, who flatter and indulge the masses and turn them into a collective "monarch" that wields the "supreme power." This monarchical "people" overrides the law and eventually turns into a "despot." A little later Aristotle describes the ultimate degeneration of such a government—revolution and civil war brought about by the "intemperance of demagogues" who, fomenting class warfare, attack men of property and "stir up the people against them." The nobles then make common cause, overthrow the democracy, and create an oligarchy. "For sometimes," Aristotle writes,

---

3. *Republic* 562d–e, 565a, trans. Jowett.

"the demagogues, in order to curry favour with the people, wrong the notables and so force them to combine—either they make a division of their property, or diminish their incomes by the imposition of public services [the "liturgies" discussed in Chapter 1], and sometimes they bring accusations against the rich so that they may have their wealth to confiscate."[4] Again political freedom is lost.

These ancient prophecies of the inevitable fate of democracy, its decline into mob rule or a tyrannical oligarchy, influenced the antidemocratic founders, who thought they saw signs of such disorder in the overly democratic state governments in the decade between the Revolution and the Constitutional Convention, in the rhetoric of class warfare rife throughout that period, and in civil unrest like Shays' Rebellion and the Fort Wilson Riot. As we saw above, their fears, like those of the ancients, were of violent revolution or civil strife brought about by the excesses of the people, which ultimately provoke a violent reaction on the part of the wronged elites, or which breed a tyrannical faction that destroys political freedom. As Fisher Ames, one of the last antidemocrats of the founding generation, wrote in 1805, "A democracy cannot last. Its nature ordains that its next change shall be into a military despotism. . . . The reason is, that the tyranny of what is called the people, and that by the sword, both operate alike to debase and corrupt, till there are neither men left with the spirit to desire liberty, nor morals with the power to sustain justice."[5]

Few of the founders, however, anticipated the more insidious and dangerous form of tyranny bred by democracy's excesses, the "softer" despotism, as Alexis de Tocqueville calls it in his famous analysis of how democracy degenerates, of a federal government grown tyrannical in its intrusive powers that are exercised through legal and regulatory coercion rather than naked force, and financed by taxes and entitlements rather than by the violent redistribution of property.[6] Yet in the end the result

---

4. *Politics* 1292a, 1304b–5a, trans. Jowett.
5. "The Dangers of American Liberty," in *The Works of Fisher Ames*, vol. 2, ed. Seth Ames (1854; Boston, 1971), 382.
6. *Democracy in America*, vol. 2, 316.

is the same—the diminution of personal autonomy, the transformation of political freedom into hedonistic license, and the growth of the encroaching and overweening power of the Leviathan state. A few decades after the Civil War, a new political movement arose that started the United States down the road to de Tocqueville's soft despotism.

Progressivism and the Expansion of the Federal Government

The Progressive movement began in the 1890s and dominated US politics until the 1920s, electing two presidents, Theodore Roosevelt and Woodrow Wilson, who despite their electoral competition nonetheless endorsed to varying degrees of emphasis the tenets of Progressivism. Yet the Progressive ideology did not end with the second term of Woodrow Wilson. For over a century its fundamental assumptions and ideas have lived on and driven the expansion and aims of the federal government under presidents of both parties, but particularly during the administrations of Democrats Franklin D. Roosevelt, Lyndon Johnson, and Barack Obama.

The core of Progressivism is a rejection of the philosophical foundations of the Constitution. The framers distrusted a human nature driven by "passions and interests," as James Madison said, whether these are found in the turbulent masses, in competing factional interests, or in an elite vulnerable to the corruption of power. The Progressives, in contrast, believed human nature could be improved under the environmental forces of technological, scientific, and economic changes. New "sciences," moreover, had developed that were discovering the material causes of human behavior whether social, economic, or political, and that were creating technical means of alleviating the social and economic disruptions attending these changes. Masters of this new knowledge and the techniques for applying it were now available for applying these insights into governing and managing the state, and solving the new problems that had arisen from industrialization and technological change. The founders' Constitution had to be replaced by the "living Constitution" that codified and empowered this new knowledge and the government based on it.

Historians Ronald J. Pestritto and William J. Atto describe the impact of this ideology on Progressive attitudes toward the Constitution and its structure of limited government and checks and balances. Progressives wanted "to enlarge vastly the scope of the national government for the purpose of responding to a set of economic and social conditions which, progressives contend, could not have been envisioned at the founding and for which the founders' limited, constitutional government was inadequate. Whereas the founders had posited what they held to be a permanent understanding of just government, based upon a permanent account of human nature, the progressives countered that the ends and scope of government were to be defined anew in each historical epoch." With their faith in social-political evolution, Progressives argued that "government was less of a danger to the governed and more capable of solving the great array of problems besetting the human race" than were local and state governments, civil society, or the free market.[7]

These ideas are explicit in the public speeches and writings of Progressive presidents Theodore Roosevelt and Woodrow Wilson. In his First Annual Message to Congress (our State of the Union speech) in 1901, Roosevelt linked historical changes to the need to adapt the Constitution to reflect them. "The tremendous and highly complex industrial development which went on with ever accelerated rapidity during the latter half of the nineteenth century brings us face to face, at the beginning of the twentieth, with very serious social problems. The old laws, and the old customs which had almost the binding force of law, were once quite sufficient to regulate the accumulation and distribution of wealth. Since the industrial changes which have so enormously increased the productive power of mankind, they are no longer sufficient."[8] Addressing the increased power of corporations over society and the economy, Roosevelt called for greater federal powers to monitor and police big business. "When the Constitution was adopted,

---

7. *American Progressivism*, eds. Ronald J. Pestritto and William J. Atto (Lanham, MD, 2008), 2–3.
8. Theodore Roosevelt's First Inaugural Message, http://www.presidency.ucsb .edu/ws/?pid=29542#ixzz2g8B5eBFz.

at the end of the eighteenth century, no human wisdom could foretell the sweeping changes, alike in industrial and political conditions, which were to take place by the beginning of the twentieth century. At that time it was accepted as a matter of course that the several States were the proper authorities to regulate, so far as was then necessary, the comparatively insignificant and strictly localized corporate bodies of the day. The conditions are now wholly different and wholly different action is called for. I believe that a law can be framed which will enable the National Government to exercise control [of corporations] along the lines above indicated."[9] The states, the people, and the market economy could not be trusted to understand and solve the various problems and dislocations brought about by economic change. An enlarged federal government armed with coercive regulatory power administered by technocrats was necessary.

Woodrow Wilson made a similar argument in Chapter 2 of his book *The New Freedom*, published in 1913. "The laws of this country," Wilson wrote, "have not kept up with the change of economic circumstances in this country; they have not kept up with the change of political circumstances." This failure to adapt is blamed on the structure of the Constitution and the time-bound assumptions of the framers. "Politics in their thought was a variety of mechanics. The Constitution was founded on the law of gravitation. The government was to exist and move by virtue of the efficacy of 'checks and balances.' The trouble with the theory is that government is not a machine, but a living thing. It falls, not under the theory of the universe, but under the theory of organic life. It is accountable to Darwin, not to Newton. It is modified by its environment, necessitated by its tasks, shaped to its functions by the sheer pressure of life. . . . All that progressives ask or desire is permission—in an era when 'development,' 'evolution,' is the scientific word—to interpret the Constitution according to the Darwinian principle; all they ask is recognition of the fact that a nation is a living thing and not a machine." Contrary to the founders' belief in a constant and corruptible human nature, the Progressives, extending Darwinian theory to society and politics, believed human

---

9. Roosevelt's First Inaugural Message.

nature is plastic, and thus is amenable to progressive improvement if the malign influences of corrupt corporations and politicians is corrected by those armed with "scientific" knowledge of human behavior.[10]

The preference for trusting technocratic administrative elites rather than Constitutional politics to run the state would seem to suggest an antidemocratic bias to Progressive ideas redolent of Plato or Socrates. Yet the rhetoric of Progressives claimed that their political ideology would lead to a purer democracy for the people, whose interests were ignored by the corrupt economic and political elites running the country. Superficially their attacks on corrupt elites and their demands for greater democracy and equality recalled the rhetoric of Thomas Jefferson and Andrew Jackson, and their denunciations of those who privileged property and wealth over the rights of the people evoked Abraham Lincoln, their presidential model and hero.

Theodore Roosevelt, for example, in his 1910 speech "The New Nationalism," said, "Our country—this great republic—means nothing unless it means the triumph of a real democracy, the triumph of popular government, and in the long run, of an economic system under which each man shall be guaranteed the opportunity to show the best that there is in him."[11] In an article a year later titled "Who Is a Progressive," Roosevelt argued, in tones redolent of the Antifederalists, against "those other men who distrust the people, and many of whom not merely distrust the people, but wish to keep them helpless so as to exploit them for their own benefit." In contrast, the Progressives "propose to do away with whatever in our government tends to secure to privilege, and to the great sinister special interests, a rampart from behind which they can beat back the forces that strive for social and industrial justice, and frustrate the will of the people."[12] Woodrow Wilson in *The New Freedom* agreed: "The government, which was designed for the people, has got into the hands of the bosses and their employers, the special interests. An invisible empire

---

10. Woodrow Wilson, *The New Freedom,* http://www.gutenberg.org/files/14811/14811-h/14811-h.htm#II.

11. In *American Progressivism*, 211.

12. In *American Progressivism*, 36.

has been set up above the forms of democracy."[13] In a speech delivered in January 1916, he asked rhetorically, "Do you never stop to reflect just what it is that America stands for? If she stands for one thing more than another, it is for the sovereignty of self-governing peoples."[14]

The class-warfare rhetoric of both presidents recalls the paeans to the people like Thomas Jefferson's praise of the "due sense of our equal right to the use of our own faculties, to the acquisitions of our own industry, to honor and confidence from our fellow-citizens, resulting not from birth, but from our actions and their sense of them."[15] It evokes the same distrust of Andrew Jackson's "moneyed aristocracy dangerous to the liberties of the country."[16] And it echoes Abraham Lincoln's attack on slave-owners who were "supplanting the principles of free government, and restoring those of classification, caste, and legitimacy."[17]

Yet behind this populist rhetoric was an understanding of democracy and the people very different from that of Jefferson, Jackson, or Lincoln. Rather than the freedom of individuals to rise as far as their talents and abilities could take them under equal laws and without hindrance from elites defined by caste, birth, or wealth, freedom for Progressives was the freedom not of particular individuals or local communities in all their variety of clashing interests and beliefs, but of an abstract collectivist "people," one that ignored the great variety of regional, sectional, and religious identities and folkways comprising the flesh-and-blood people of the United States. Now those various interests and aims would be homogenized and unified according to the interests, values, and aims as defined and chosen by techno-political elites.

----

13. Wilson, *The New Freedom*.
14. Woodrow Wilson, 1916 speech, http://books.google.com/books?id=-rIqA AAAYAAJ&pg=RA9-PA11&dq=PITTSBURGH#v=onepage&q=PITTS BURGH&f=false.
15. Thomas Jefferson's First Inaugural Address http://avalon.law.yale.edu/19th _century/jefinau1.asp.
16. In Remini, *The Legacy of Andrew Jackson*, 14.
17. In *The Collected Works of Abraham Lincoln*, 376.

Theodore Roosevelt in his "New Nationalism" speech suggested this more collective view of the people in his claim that an individual right such as the right to property can be limited by the "community" through government "interference," according to the values of the "advocate of human welfare, who rightly maintains that every man holds his property subject to the general right of the community to regulate its use to whatever degree the public welfare may require it." Roosevelt later allows an individual the right to create "wealth" with his "power and sagacity," but adds, only "when exercised with entire regard to the welfare of his fellows," and when his gaining this wealth "represents a benefit to the community." These comments are similarly followed by his asserting the need for a "policy of a far more active government interference with social and economic conditions." Enforcing this regulatory "interference," moreover, is the responsibility of the federal government, which alone embodies the "people": "The national government belongs to the whole American people, and where the whole American people are interested, that interest can be guarded effectively only by the national government. The betterment which we seek must be accomplished, I believe, mainly through the national government."[18] In his eighth Annual Message to Congress, he asserted, "The danger to American democracy lies not in the least in the concentration of administrative power in responsible and accountable hands. It lies in having the power insufficiently concentrated, so that no one can be held responsible to the people for its use."[19]

Woodrow Wilson similarly evoked this redefinition of the "people" in his belief that "society is a living organism" and as such justifies his "Darwinian" view of the Constitution and its need to "develop." A few pages later in *The New Freedom* he writes more explicitly about the shift of focus from individuals to the larger social organism. Imagining the progressive utopia that will come into being once the existing politico-social order has been rebuilt by what Wilson calls political "architects" and

---

18. In *American Progressivism*, 217, 220–21.
19. In Paul D. Moreno, *The American State from the Civil War to the New Deal* (Cambridge, England, 2013), 113.

"engineers," he describes it as a structure "where men can live as a single community, co-operative as in a perfected, co-ordinated [sic] beehive."[20] Apart from the whiff of totalitarian, antihumanist collectivism in such rhetoric, the important questions are who gets to define this unitary collective "interest" or "benefit," and why the state governments or civil society, closer to the variety of interests and beliefs among the people, are not better placed—and more directly accountable—than a far-off central government and political "engineers" to address more efficiently and specifically these varied and necessarily conflicting interests.

Such paeans to collectivism were even more explicit in social worker and Progressive theorist Mary Parker Follett's 1918 book *The New State*. "Man can have no rights apart from society or independent of society or against society," Follett wrote. The individual rights granted by "Nature and Nature's God," as Thomas Jefferson wrote, should be augmented by "social rights," which are potentially unlimited. "Our efforts are to be bent not upon guarding the rights which Heaven has showered upon us, but in creating all the rights we shall ever have." The agent of this expansion of rights must be the state: "The state has a higher function than either restraining individuals or protecting individuals. It is to have a great forward policy which shall follow the collective will of the people, a collective will which embodied through our state, in our life, shall be the basis of progress yet undreamed of." This powerful state necessitates a redefinition of democracy, which now comprises not a multiplicity of individuals or factions and their warring "passions and interests," but a "great spiritual unity which is supported by the most vital trend in philosophical thought and by the latest biologists and social psychologists. . . . Democracy is every one building the single life, not my life and others, not the individual and the state, but my life bound up with others, the individual which *is* the state, the state which *is* the individual."[21]

This collectivist understanding of the "people" was also asserted by the influential theorists of Progressivism, whose notions of "social

---

20. Wilson, *The New Freedom*.
21. In *The Social and Political Thought of American Progressivism*, ed. Eldon J. Eisenach (Indianapolis, 2006), 33–35, 37. Emphases in original.

justice" included a more equitable distribution of property. Herbert Croly was a cofounder of *The New Republic* magazine, and his 1909 book *The Promise of American Life* was endorsed by Supreme Court Justice Felix Frankfurter as "the most powerful single contribution to progressive thinking."[22] In that book Croly asserted, "The people are not Sovereign as individuals. They are not Sovereign in reason and morals even when united into a majority. They become Sovereign only in so far as they succeed in reaching and expressing a collective purpose."[23] And he is forthright about what that "collective purpose" entails: "In becoming responsible for the subordination of the individual to the demand of a dominant and constructive national purpose, the American state will in effect be making itself responsible for a morally and socially desirable distribution of wealth."[24] Five years later, in *Progressive Democracy* (1914) Croly again defined democracy in terms of a "people" who pursue not a multitude of conflicting "passions and interests," as Madison believed, but a "collective purpose": "Direct democracy . . . has little meaning except in a community which is resolutely pursuing a vigorous social program. It must become one of a group of political institutions, whose object is fundamentally to invigorate and socialize the action of American public opinion."

Moreover, achieving goals like a "vigorous social program" or a "collective purpose" requires a bigger federal government: "The realization of a genuine social policy necessitates the aggrandizement of the administrative and legislative branches of the government," though Croly does admit the need for "direct popular supervision."[25] Such expansion requires as well a conception of individual rights far different from that of the Constitution. Another influential progressive theorist, Frank Johnson Goodnow, a law professor at Columbia University and later president of Johns Hopkins, in 1916 wrote, "Changed conditions . . .

---

22. In Jonah Goldberg, *Liberal Fascism* (New York, 2007), 97.
23. Herbert Croly, *The Promise of American Life*, http://www.gutenberg.org/files /14422/14422-h/14422-h.htm#CHAPTER_IX.
24. Herbert Croly, http://www.gutenberg.org/files/14422/14422-h/14422-h.htm #CHAPTER_I.
25. In *American Progressivism*, 243–44.

must bring in their train different conceptions of private rights if society is to be advantageously carried on." Old notions of individual rights, though suitable for their times, "may become a menace when social rather than individual efficiency is the necessary prerequisite of progress. For social efficiency probably owes more to the common realization of social duties than to the general insistence on privileges based on individual private rights." Thus "man under modern conditions is primarily a member of society" and "only as he recognizes his duties as a member of society can he secure the greatest opportunities as an individual."[26] Historian Charles Beard—whose 1913 study *The Economic Interpretation of the Constitution of the United States* is the most famous argument for the theory that the Constitution was fashioned to serve the property and business interests of an elite at the expense of the people—was even more forthright in his skepticism of individual rights. In 1912 he wrote, "The doctrine that the individual has fundamental personal and property rights which are beyond the reach, not only of the majority but of the state itself, can be sustained on no other theory than that of anarchy. It rests upon a notion as obsolete and indefensible as the doctrine of natural rights."[27]

This collective "people," in the view of the Progressives, can be served only by the federal government, especially a powerful executive and the various bureaucracies and agencies that would have to be created in order to implement the new policies and regulations necessary for achieving the "social justice," "social duties," and "social efficiency" that presumably comprise the true interests of the people, whether they know it or not. Central to this more expansive power was the need for a more "scientific" administrative organization of an increasing number of federal agencies. According to Croly in *The Promise of American Life*, "Only by faith in an efficient national organization, and by an exclusive and aggressive devotion to the national welfare, can the American democratic ideal be made good." After admitting the need to monitor the federal government and allowing a role for state and municipal govern-

---

26. From *The American Conception of Liberty*, in *American Progressivism*, 62–63.
27. In Bernard C. Borning, *The Political and Social Thought of Charles A. Beard* (1962; Westport, CT, 1984), 76. In Moreno, 112.

ments, Croly adds, "under existing conditions and simply as a matter of expediency, the national advance of the American democracy does demand an increasing amount of centralized action and responsibility." Such a change would need, of course, to discard the "strong, almost dominant, tendency to regard the existing Constitution with superstitious awe, and to shrink with horror from modifying it even in the smallest detail. . . . If such an abject worship of legal precedent for its own sake should continue, the American idea will have to be fitted to the rigid and narrow lines of a few legal formulas."[28]

Obviously, Croly endorses the assumption that social reality and human nature have evolved beyond the Founders' belief in the eternal, conflicting "passions and interests" that the Constitution checked and balanced institutionally in order to protect both the freedom of minorities from oppression by the masses, and the freedom of the masses from oppression by an elite minority.

Woodrow Wilson similarly was concerned with the "science of administration" that could instruct federal administrators in the techniques for creating, instituting, and managing the requisite policies. In his essay "The Study of Administration," published in 1887, Wilson asserted that administration—not, as the founders believed, protecting individual freedom—was the most important function of government: "it is government in action; it is the executive, the operative, the most visible side of government." Yet no science of administration has been created to define its techniques and methods. Such a science is necessary because the new economic and technological changes have multiplied the functions of government: "There is scarcely a single duty of government which was once simple which is not now complex." The people now demand greater government participation in economic life, "steadily widening to new conceptions of state duty; so that, at the same time that the functions of government are every day becoming more complex and difficult, they are also vastly multiplying in number. Administration is everywhere putting its hands to new undertakings. . . .

---

28. Croly, http://www.gutenberg.org/files/14422/14422-h/14422-h.htm#CHAP
    TER_IX.

Whatever holds of authority state or federal governments are to take upon corporations, there must follow cares and responsibilities which will require not a little wisdom, knowledge, and experience. Such things must be studied in order to be well done."

The practical aim of such study will be to "open for the public a bureau of skilled, economical administration," comprising the "hundreds who are wise" empowered to guide the thousands who are "selfish, ignorant, timid, stubborn, or foolish," the latter phrase a clue to the Progressives' patronizing estimation of the "people." As a "science," then, administration "lies outside the proper sphere of *politics.* Administrative questions are not political questions. Although politics sets the tasks for administration, it should not be suffered to manipulate its offices."[29] In his emphasis on the federal administration, Wilson, like other Progressives, recognized only the federal government and the indiscriminate mass of the "people" unable to know their own interests. The Progressives and their political heirs ignored and then actively displaced the numerous other nongovernmental mediating organizations and associations—families, churches, mutual-aid societies, fraternal societies, voluntary associations—that addressed many of the social problems the Progressives decried.

The ideal of an apolitical cadre of technocrats managing the state may sound similar to the antidemocratic founders' notion of republican "filters" tempering the passions of the turbulent masses. But such legislative and executive "filters" were superior mainly because of wisdom, practical experience, and virtue, not necessarily technical knowledge. At least in theory, they would emerge through a process of "filtration" by their local communities and states. And in the Constitution, they were directly or indirectly selected by the people through the franchise and subjected to term limits, and thus to some measure accountable. They were also the people actually publicly debating and making policy, unlike the unelected legions of anonymous "technicians" in government bureaus and agencies who flesh out with specific policies and regulations the general aims in any congressional legislation.

---

29. In *American Progressivism*, 192, 194–95, 199, 201. Emphasis in original.

Most important, for all the Progressive talk of expressing the peoples' "interests," now these interests do not arise from the people and are directly or indirectly communicated to their representatives, but are selected and imposed upon them by distant and presumably wiser others. As Wilson put it, "Whoever would effect a change in a modern constitutional government must first educate his fellow-citizens to *want* some change. That done, he must persuade them to want the particular change he wants. He must first make public opinion willing to listen and then see to it that it listen to the right things. He must stir it up to search for an opinion, and then manage to put the right opinion in its way."[30] This faith in an administrative elite that can divine the people's interests of which they are not even aware is a far cry from the beliefs of Jefferson, Jackson, or Lincoln. Those democratic champions had faith in the common sense and ability of the average person in the United States to know his own interests, as long as he was free politically to do so without interference from self-selected, corrupt elites, particularly those in the federal government.

In contrast, the Progressives discarded the universal distrust of elites *of any sort* who are insulated from political accountability, the suspicion found in both the Federalists and their democratic critics like Jefferson and Jackson. Progressives, on the contrary, believed that alleged advances in the "human sciences" such as sociology or psychology had created knowledge and techniques that insulated technocrats and their political masters from the inevitable temptation to abuse power assumed to be a permanent feature of human nature by political philosophers from ancient Athens to the framers. In contrast to such traditional wisdom, as Progressive journalist Walter Lippmann wrote in 1914, "We can no longer treat life as something that has trickled down to us. We have to deal with it deliberately, devise its social organization, alter its tools, formulate its method, educate and control it. In endless ways we put intention where custom has reigned. We break up routines, make decisions, choose our ends, select means." Such activism is possible because "the great triumph of modern psychology is

---

30. In *American Progressivism*, 200. Emphasis in original.

its growing capacity for penetrating to the desires that govern our thought."[31]

Progressives, that is, are in possession of "scientific" knowledge about human nature unavailable to the founders, and can use that knowledge to alter human nature in order to improve social life. But in their unexamined assumptions that such political and moral progress had indeed taken place, and that the "human sciences" were indeed as rigorous, accurate, and predictive as natural science, the Progressives forgot the monitory question of the Roman satirist Juvenal: "Who will guard the guardians?"

Finally, the belief in expanding administrative elites was accompanied with a call for a more powerful and vigorous president who could better embody the "will of the people" and direct the agencies effecting it than are the state governments and the legislative branch, which comprise numerous clashing "passions and interests" that obscure the collective people's genuine interests and well-being as these are discerned by "experts." In the 1920 edition of his autobiography, Theodore Roosevelt described the president as the "steward of the people," empowered "to do anything that the needs of the nation demanded unless such action was forbidden by the Constitution or the laws." As he further explained, "I did not usurp power, but I did greatly broaden the use of executive power."[32] In practice, Roosevelt's obeisance to the Constitution was more flexible. His interference in the Anthracite Coal Strike of 1902 elicited concerns that he was overstepping the constitutional limits on the executive. When the Republican whip James E. Watson pointed this out to Roosevelt, he replied, "The Constitution was made for the people, and not the people for the Constitution." According to Watson's memoirs, when pressed on the matter Roosevelt shouted, "To hell with the Constitution when the people want coal!"[33]

---

31. In Eisenach, 258. Lippmann later acknowledged the totalitarian dangers of statism in his 1937 book *The Good Society*.
32. *The Autobiography of Theodore Roosevelt*, ed. Wayne Andrews (New York, 1958), 197, 198.
33. In Moreno, 89–90.

Woodrow Wilson held similar views on the role of the president and his need to be a "leader of men," the title of Wilson's 1890 essay. Rather than the Constitution's limited executive, Wilson envisions a more activist president who has "such sympathetic and penetrative insight as shall enable him to discern quite unerringly the motives which move other men *in the mass*. . . . It need not pierce the particular secrets of *individual* men: it need only know what it is that lies waiting to be stirred in the minds and purposes of groups and masses of men. Besides, it is not a sympathy that serves, but a sympathy whose power is to command, to command by knowing its instrument. . . . The competent leader of men cares little for the interior niceties of other people's characters: he cares much-everything [sic] for the external uses to which they may be put. His will seeks the lines of least resistance; but the whole question with him is a question *of the application of force*. There are men to be moved: how shall he move them?"[34]

Years later in the *Constitutional Government in the United States*, published in 1908, Wilson is explicit that the sort of leader he believes necessary would be politically embodied in a president more powerful than the Constitution's chief executive, who was limited to being "only the legal executive, the presiding and guiding authority in the application of law and the execution of policy. . . . He was empowered [by the veto] to prevent bad laws, but he was not to be given an opportunity to make good ones." Wilson apparently forgot that the Constitution gives Congress the authority to make laws. In further contrast to the constitutional order, Wilson posits that government "is a living, organic thing, and must, like every other government, work out the close synthesis of active parts, which exist only when leadership is lodged in some one man or group of men." And directly contradicting the Constitution's structure based on balancing and checking clashing "passions and interests," Wilson writes, "You cannot compound a successful government out of antagonisms." Thus we must "look to the President as the unifying force in our complex system, the leader both of his party and of the

---

34. Woodrow Wilson, "Leaders of Men," http://teachingamericanhistory.org/library /document/leaders-of-men. Emphases in original.

nation."[35] Power concentrated in the federal government required a proactive, dynamic executive in order to create the national consensus necessary for reform.

The Tools of Leviathan

A powerful president overseeing an expansive federal government of agencies and commissions requires money to achieve his utopian aims. And in keeping with antidemocratic fears dating back to ancient Athens, revenue seized or collected from the rich could be redistributed to the poor, a goal explicit in the more radical Progressives' class-warfare and egalitarian rhetoric.

At the 1912 convention of the short-lived Progressive or "Bull Moose" Party, formed by Theodore Roosevelt after his split with the Republican president William Howard Taft, former Indiana senator Albert Beveridge sounded these class-warfare and redistributionist themes in his keynote speech. Contrasting "social brotherhood" with "savage individualism," and "intelligent co-operation" with "reckless competition," Beveridge called for "equal rights as a fact of life instead of a catch-word [sic] of politics." Like Progressives of all stripes, Beveridge championed a collectivist "people" and called for removing the constitutional "filters"— selection of senators by the states, and election of the president by the Electoral College—that empowered corrupt political elites. And endorsing the utopian aims of the Progressives, Beveridge thundered, "There ought not to be in this Republic a single day of bad business, a single unemployed workman, a single unfed child," nor should US workmen ever know "a day of low wages, idleness or want." Greater government control of business was one way to achieve these boons—"We aim to put new business laws on our statute books which will tell American businessmen what they can do and what they cannot do." Redistribution of property would be the most important mechanism for realizing these aims: "We mean not only to make prosperity steady," Beveridge orated,

---

35. In *American Progressivism*, 156–57. See Goldberg, *Liberal Fascism*, 78–120, for how Wilson's presidency embodied these ideas.

"but to give to the many who earn it a just share of that prosperity instead of helping the few who do not earn it to take an unjust share. The Progressive motto is 'Pass the prosperity around,'" a sentiment President Obama would echo in October 2008 when he said, "I think when you spread the wealth around, it's good for everybody."[36]

The Sixteenth Amendment, which in 1913 instituted a national income tax, would become the means of taking money from the rich and redistributing it to the rest through various government programs. At first the tax exempted income under $3,000 ($70,872 in 2013 dollars) and set the top rate at 7 percent on incomes over $500,000 (almost $12 million in 2013 dollars), making it attractive to citizens who thought only the super-rich would be affected. But World War I created the rationale for increasing the reach of the income tax. The 1916 Revenue Act doubled most income tax rates of the Sixteenth Amendment to a top rate of 13 percent, along with creating an inheritance tax. *The New Republic* called it "a powerful equalitarian attack upon swollen incomes." The 1917 Tax Act "lowered income-tax exemptions and raised rates, the top rate to 67 percent and 77 percent in 1918," Moreno writes. The Progressive economist E. R. A. Seligman thought this revenue legislation revealed "the progress that has been made in the conception of fiscal justice as a result of the democratic development of the last generation."[37]

In addition to instituting an income tax to finance a burgeoning federal government, the Progressives exploited the national populist mood to weaken federalism by removing one of the most important prerogatives of state sovereignty, the election of senators. The Seventeenth Amendment, ratified in 1913, called for the popular election of senators, thus eliminating one of the constitutional "filters" on the power of the masses and the federal government alike. Bribery, corruption, and legislative deadlock in the selection of senators by the states were the arguments for this change, but class envy and populist suspicion of plutocratic

---

36. In *The Birth of the New Party or Progressive Democracy*, ed. George Henry Payne (Naperville, IL, 1912), 283, 288–90, 294. Barrack Obama, http://www.tampabay.com/news/perspective/joe-the-plumber-a-transcript/858299.

37. Moreno, 166.

elites contributed to the groundswell of support for the amendment. The change also expressed the Progressive belief in greater "democracy," and in the notion that the structures of the Constitution were outmoded now that Americans were "a new people living and acting under an old system," as Indiana senator David Turpie said during the debate on the amendment.[38]

As a result of the passage of the Seventeenth Amendment, the power of the states, an important check on the "encroaching power" of the central government, was seriously weakened. But as historian Ralph A. Rossum writes, the threat to federalism was scarcely mentioned in the debates over the amendment. One eloquent exception was Elihu Root, a Republican senator from New York. During the debate over the amendment Root correctly prophesized, "The time will come when the Government of the United States will be driven to the exercise of more arbitrary and unconsidered power, will be driven to greater concentration, will be driven to extend its functions into the internal affairs of the States."[39] But for Progressives, their belief in the "evolving" Constitution and their championing of the abstract "people" rendered this reservation anachronistic. More important to them was the need to remove the political structures such as federalism and the powers of the states, which mediated between the volatile masses and the centralized government in Washington, thus checking the power of the latter.

The political philosophy of the Progressives, despite their protestations of admiration for Abraham Lincoln and the founders, "aimed at the foundation of a new political regime," as Paul Rahe writes, "distinct from and, in certain critical respects, opposed to the one that had gradually taken shape in the period stretching from 1776 to 1789." The Progressives, Rahe continues, in fact abandoned Lincoln, Jefferson, and Hamilton, "dismissing as outdated the concern with individual, natural rights that the three men shared; rejecting as wrongheaded and outmoded Jefferson's argument for the virtues of political jealousy and his

---

38. In Ralph A. Rossum, *Federalism, The Supreme Court, and the Seventeenth Amendment* (Lanham, MD, 2001), 191.
39. In Rossum, 202.

insistence that vigorous local self-government is essential to the maintenance of liberty; and substituting for Hamilton's notion of statesman-
ship and for that of Lincoln an account . . . which was incompatible with
the principle of limited government and closely akin in its practical aspects
to the vision of rational administration" proposed by French political philosophers like Turgot.[40]

For all their rhetoric of "pure democracy" and the "people's welfare," then, the Progressives were in embryo a modern version of the
ancient tyrants who championed the people in order to aggrandize their
own power, which they financed by redistributing property. Under
the pressures and crises of two world wars and the Great Depression,
the expansion of the federal Leviathan through the proliferation of
agencies and regulations would be accompanied by the multiplication of
social welfare programs that, for all their initial good intentions, would
evolve into the modern equivalent of the redistribution of property with
which the ancient tyrant bought the support of the masses. The high
price would be the erosion of personal freedom and self-government by
coercive federal regulatory power over more and more of private and state
business.

FDR and the Growth of Entitlement Democracy

As they promised, the early Progressives expanded the federal administration to exert control over corporations and the economy. Under
Woodrow Wilson, the 1914 Federal Trade Commission, for example,
increased federal regulatory and investigative power over business in
order to manage competition and enforce antitrust laws. The Federal
Reserve Board, created by the 1913 Federal Reserve Act, increased regulations over banking and the money supply. As Moreno writes, both
agencies "would in time acquire tremendous policymaking power and
pose serious constitutional questions."[41] Once the United States entered
World War I in 1917, the pace of centralization, collectivization, and

---

40. *Soft Despotism*, 245–46.
41. Moreno, 144.

expansion of federal power quickened. "Novel boards and agencies," political philosopher Robert Nisbet writes, "were fashioned to assimilate the whole American economic and social fabric in their workings." The War Industries Board, the War Labor Policies Boards, the Shipping Board, the Food Administration, and, Nisbet adds, "before the ending of the war many another centralized, national authority [was] created by the Congress or the executive in which absolute power was vested in its own sphere." Personal freedom was compromised as well by the 1917 Espionage Act and the 1918 Sedition Act, under which almost two hundred thousand people "were accused, or indicted, or found guilty and fined heavily or imprisoned for remarks heard or overheard in public." Yet consistent with the ancient predictions of democratic tyranny financed and softened by wealth transfers to the people, Nisbet continues, "Lost neighborhood, local, and other liberties didn't seem too high a price to pay for the economic benefits in the form of high wages, props to unionism, quick and generally favorable arbitration agreements for workers, and the novel availability of spendable money, cash in hand."[42]

Though many of these federal institutions and powers would end with the war, under Woodrow Wilson a model of massive state control over social, political, and economic life had been established. Franklin Delano Roosevelt's New Deal continued this expansion, creating numerous new federal agencies and regulatory powers, and refurbishing many of Wilson's wartime measures, such as the 1917 Trading with the Enemy Act, in order to deal with the crisis of the Great Depression.

In the main, Roosevelt's policies demonstrated a broad sympathy with many Progressive ideals, for all he was an old-style partisan politician. For example, Roosevelt believed that "the age of enlightened administration has come," and that government should now turn to the business of "modifying and controlling our economic units" and of "adjusting production to consumption, of distributing wealth and products more equitably, of adapting existing economic organizations to the service of the people," though "it may in some measure qualify the

---

42. *The Present Age* (Indianapolis, IN, 1988), 45–46, 48.

freedom of action of individual units within the business," and "the re-definition of these rights in terms of a changing and growing social order," as he told San Francisco's Commonwealth Club in 1932.[43]

These views were predicated on the class-warfare assumptions that had served Theodore Roosevelt and Woodrow Wilson so well. In his first Inaugural Address in 1933, Roosevelt thundered against the "practices of the unscrupulous money changers" who "know only the rules of a generation of self-seekers." The 1936 Democratic platform more explicitly warned, "We shall continue to use the powers of government to end the activities of the malefactors of great wealth who defraud and exploit the people."[44] In his speech at the 1936 convention, Roosevelt concurred, thundering against "the privileged princes of these new economic dynasties, thirsting for power," who "created a new despotism and wrapped it in the robes of legal sanction. In its service new mercenaries sought to regiment the people, their labor, and their property." Roosevelt's rhetoric explicitly called for new "Minutemen" to battle the big-business George III and start a second American Revolution.[45] Finally, to achieve this revolution Roosevelt endorsed the Progressive preference for an "evolving" Constitution and a powerful executive necessary for achieving these aims: "It is to be hoped that the normal balance of Executive and legislative authority may be wholly adequate to meet the unprecedented task before us. But it may be that an unprecedented demand and need for undelayed action may call for temporary departure from that normal balance of public procedure."[46]

Enjoying a Democratic majority in the 73rd Congress, in his first term Roosevelt did not need to disrupt the constitutional "normal balance." That would come in 1937 with his failed attempt to pack the Supreme Court with

43. Franklin D. Roosevelt, campaign address, http://www.presidency.ucsb.edu/ws/?pid=88391#axzz2fkyxDHJY.

44. Democratic Party Platform of 1936, http://www.presidency.ucsb.edu/ws/index.php?pid=29596#axzz2jRPpY6RQ.

45. Roosevelt, acceptance speech for renomination, http://www.presidency.ucsb.edu/ws/?pid=15314#axzz2jd7pnWIS.

46. Roosevelt's First Inaugural Address, http://millercenter.org/president/speeches/detail/3280.

appointees sympathetic to his legislation. During his first term he made good on his promised activism with a flurry of legislation and executive orders. The Agricultural Adjustment Act, the Tennessee Valley Authority, the National Industrial Recovery Act comprising the National Recovery Administration (ruled unconstitutional in 1935) and the Public Works Administration, the Banking Act that created the Federal Deposit Insurance Corporation and the provisions known as the Glass-Steagall Act and the National Recovery Review Board, are the major expansions of regulatory power enacted by Roosevelt during the "hundred days" of his first term. To manage all these agencies, the federal bureaucracy had to grow by 45 percent.[47] As Roosevelt later boasted to Congress in 1936, "We have built up new instruments of public power. In the hands of a people's government this power is wholesome and proper. But in the hands of political puppets of an economic autocracy such power would provide shackles for the liberties of the people."[48] The question of how a powerful elite of unelected, unaccountable government bureaucrats would be more immune than plutocrats to the corrupting influence of "public power" is answered by the Progressive appeal to the oversight of an abstract, collectivized "people" whose interests have already been determined for them by Progressives.

By the end of the Roosevelt presidency, the concentrated power of "big government" feared by the framers of the Constitution had become the status quo in the United States, justified by crises like war and the Great Depression, and facilitated after 1937 by an emasculated Supreme Court, seven of whose members had been appointed by Roosevelt at the time of his death in 1945. Thus the Progressive ideology fulfilled one half of the ancient formula for democratic despotism—the concentration of coercive federal power, and its greater intrusion into and regulation of social and economic life.

Also under Roosevelt, the other half, the redistribution of property to secure the support of the "people," began its relentless reach and expansion, beginning in the second half of his first term with his "second

---

47. Moreno, 304.
48. In Goldberg, *Liberal Fascism*, 158.

New Deal." Unlike in antiquity, however, when critics of democracy made the "poor" the beneficiaries of the tyrant's appropriation of wealth, in the United States the middle class, and even the corporations frequently demonized by Progressives, also have become the recipients of federal largesse. Moreover, despite the transformation of Constitutional structures wrought by New Deal legislation, Roosevelt spoke the soothing language of "rights" familiar from the Constitution. In his 1935 State of the Union address, Roosevelt said that his "new order of things" was developed "under the framework and in the spirit and intent of the American Constitution."[49] By using such rhetoric, as political philosopher William Voegeli writes, Roosevelt suggested that "the New Deal was the adaptation of America's founding principles to the nation's new economic circumstances. As such, the New Deal's consequences could be dramatic, while its intentions were presented as benign or even conservative."[50]

This redefinition of "rights" became an important mechanism for creating and camouflaging Tocqueville's "soft despotism" by removing the social opprobrium traditionally attached to taking charity. We saw above Progressive Mary Parker Follett in 1918 move beyond the notion of natural rights bestowed by "Nature and Nature's God," and call for "creating all the rights we shall ever have." Roosevelt too, in his 1932 Commonwealth Club speech, made a similar claim when he spoke of "the re-definition of these rights in terms of a changing and growing social order." Now included in the list of "rights" for each citizen were "the right to make a comfortable living" and the "right to be assured . . . in the safety of his savings." Four years later in his acceptance speech at the Democratic convention, Roosevelt expanded the constitutional "right to life" to a broader right to "make a living—a living decent according to the standard of the time, a living which gives man not only enough to live by, but something to live for."[51]

In his 1944 State of the Union address, Roosevelt described even more specifically the new rights he believed should be codified in law. The

---

49. In Moreno, 258.
50. *Never Enough* (2010; New York, 2012), 74.
51. Roosevelt, acceptance speech for renomination.

rights vouchsafed by the Constitution, Roosevelt argued, "proved inadequate to assure us equality in the pursuit of happiness" under the stresses created by an "industrialized economy." In these conditions, "true individual freedom cannot exist without economic security and independence." Echoing the language of the Declaration of Independence, Roosevelt called for another founding: "In our day these economic truths have become accepted as self-evident. We have accepted, so to speak, a second Bill of Rights under which a new basis of security and prosperity can be established for all regardless of station, race, or creed."[52]

Roosevelt's compendium of these new "rights" comprised not natural rights as the founders understood them, the defining constituents of a human nature that precede any government and exist apart from its control, but benefits and goods people want and that in an imperfect world must in the main depend on their own efforts, talents, virtues, or luck, and on the help of family, friends, and local communities: a "useful and remunerative job," "adequate food and clothing and recreation," a "decent home," "adequate medical care and the opportunity to achieve and enjoy good health," "adequate protection from the economic fears of old age, sickness, accident, and unemployment," and the right "to a good education." But as William Voegeli points out, the hard question is "not about what welfare rights include, but what they exclude." Once people make a "decent life" a right, "on what basis," Voegeli asks, "can we tell people who repeatedly demand additions to the honor roll that some things are indeed conducive to a decent life but, at the same time, are not rights?"[53]

In practice, the only limit to such "rights" will be the subjective preferences, desires, tastes, and imagination of the people, no matter how extravagant, irrational, immoral, or fiscally unsustainable. And as the past seven decades have shown, the definition of "adequate," "decent," or "independence" will constantly expand as the baseline for material well-being relentlessly rises. Finally, genuine freedom and equality are both

---

52. "FDR's Second Bill of Rights," http://www.heritage.org/initiatives/first
    -principles/primary-sources/fdrs-second-bill-of-rights.
53. Voegeli, 91.

eroded when one looks to the government to define one's happiness, and then to take responsibility for providing it. In contrast, as Paul Rahe writes of the founders' understanding of liberty and equality, "Liberty consisted to a considerable degree in taking responsibility for one's own well-being and for that of one's family. It was in possessing this liberty and in being saddled with this responsibility that men were deemed equal, and it was their possession of this liberty and the allocation to them of this responsibility that government was established to protect."[54]

This expansion of entitlements to satisfy these new "rights" started with Roosevelt's Social Security Act of 1935, "a major step forward," Moreno writes, "in centralized bureaucratic statism." In 1937, the Supreme Court upheld the constitutionality of the act in two 5–4 decisions justifying the law on the grounds of the federal government's power to tax. Dissenting Justice Pierce Butler presciently wrote that the decision sanctioned the federal government to "induce, if indeed not to compel, state enactments for any purpose within the realm of state power, and generally to control state administration of state laws."[55] The role of state sovereignty in checking the power and reach of the federal government had again been considerably diminished.

The Social Security Act also set the pattern for the inevitable expansion of such programs, which in turn further increased the size and power of the federal government. In addition to providing old-age assistance, the act provided for unemployment compensation, aid to dependent children (replaced in 1996 by the Temporary Assistance to Needy Families program), maternal and child welfare, and public health work. States were compelled to participate in funding these programs, aided by grants from the federal government, yet another insidious erosion of state autonomy, since accepting the funds required accepting the federal government's control.

Over the years more and more beneficiaries were added to the Social Security program. The growth of Social Security makes it the original paradigm of the inevitable expansion of such entitlements in the cost

54. *Soft Despotism, Democracy's Drift*, 261.
55. Moreno, 258, 294.

and number of beneficiaries once they become law and are understood to be "rights." In 1939, spouses and minor children were added as beneficiaries. In 1950, benefits for the permanently disabled were signed into law. In 1956, Social Security Disability Insurance was expanded to workers between fifty and sixty-five years old, and for children disabled before the age of eighteen. In 1958, benefits were added for children of the disabled, and in 1960, age restrictions were eliminated, making anyone eligible for benefits. In 1972, state programs providing income for the blind and disabled were federalized in the Supplemental Security Income program. In 1975, cost-of-living increases for beneficiaries were authorized, and in 1997 the State Children's Health Insurance Program for low-income citizens or "CHIPS" program was created.

In subsequent presidencies, more and more programs have sprung up to recognize more and more "rights," at the same time they function as a mechanism to redistribute income; as F. A. Hayek wrote of Social Security, "No system of monopolistic insurance has resisted this transformation into something quite different, an instrument for the compulsory redistribution of income" and "a tool of egalitarian redistribution."[56] The next significant expansion came in Lyndon Johnson's Great Society legislation, which institutionalized a whole catalogue of utopian progressive goals. The War on Poverty legislation included the Economic Opportunity Act of 1964, which created eleven major programs. These included funding for education and job training, once the responsibility of states and private enterprise. The Food Stamp Act subsidized food purchases. The Social Security Act of 1965 created Medicare, which subsidizes health care for the elderly, and Title XIX of that act created Medicaid, which expanded that support to everyone below the poverty threshold. Social Security benefits and eligibility requirements were once again liberalized in the Social Security Amendments of 1965 and 1967. The latter also liberalized Medicaid requirements. In addition, the Great Society created and funded "cultural" programs such as the National Endowment for the Arts, the National Endowment for the Humanities, and the Corporation for Public Broadcast-

---

56. In *The Constitution of Liberty* (1960; Chicago, 2011), 409–10.

ing, extending the federal government's regulatory reach into the arts and entertainment.

Over the last half-century, new entitlements, along with new federal agencies and regulations, have continued to be created and existing ones expanded under administrations of both parties. Indeed, according to economist Nicholas Eberstadt, in any given year the growth of entitlement spending has been over 8 percent higher under Republican administrations.[57] Republican George W. Bush in 2003 signed into law the Medicare Prescription Drug, Improvement, and Modernization Act, which increased subsidizes for purchasing medications. Through 2012 the program has added $318 billion to the national debt, as the act had no dedicated funding.[58] And Democrat Barack Obama in 2010 created the Affordable Care Act, which aims to provide health care to the 47 million people in the United States who are uninsured, in addition to imposing even more federal regulations over an industry representing one-sixth of the whole economy. According to the Heritage Foundation, this program will cost $1.8 trillion over the next decade, while collecting $500 billion in new taxes.[59] Once created, programs such as these have been renamed, reconfigured, or replaced, but hardly ever eliminated, even as new programs are created to gratify "rights," the term used to denominate what used to be called "charity" or "hand-outs."[60]

Moreover, all classes, not just the poor, are beneficiaries of these and other transfers through tax deductions and credits, such as the home-mortgage deduction or the Coverdell educational savings accounts, or direct government wealth distribution through programs like agricultural subsidies, or federal loans and loan guarantees subsidizing US exporters, home buyers, or college tuition. Many recipients do not con-

---

57. In *A Nation of Takers* (West Conshohocken, PA, 2012), 23.
58. See http://www.cms.gov/Research-Statistics-Data-and-Systems/Statistics-Trends -and-Reports/ReportsTrustFunds/Downloads/TR2013.pdf.
59. Alyene Senger, "Obamacare's Impact on Today's and Tomorrow's Taxpayers," http://www.heritage.org/research/reports/2013/08/obamacares-impact-on -todays-and-tomorrows-taxpayers-an-update.
60. One exception is the 1988 Medicare Catastrophic Coverage Act, which was repealed sixteen months later.

sider these programs redistributive transfers like welfare or food stamps, and so they have a huge interested constituency that protects them from elimination and makes even modest reductions politically difficult. As Voegeli points out, "The welfare state was shrewdly designed to summon into existence permanent political forces that would favor the welfare state's expansion and oppose its contraction. The ideal is for every US household to consider itself, correctly or incorrectly, a net importer of dollars after the welfare state has extracted all its taxes and conferred all its benefits."[61] As a result, reducing entitlement programs, let alone reforming them, is politically toxic for anyone seeking federal office.

Over the last century, the size and costs of the federal Leviathan and its mechanisms for redistributing wealth have become staggering, as has the number of people receiving benefits. As of January 2012, the federal government employed 2.3 million workers, excluding military personnel, at a cost of $200 billion a year.[62] Total federal spending in 2013 was $3.5 trillion, a 40 percent increase over the last decade. Equally significant is the intrusive, coercive regulatory apparatus that has followed this expansion of the federal government under both parties. Republican Richard Nixon, for example, in 1970 created by executive order the Environmental Protection Agency, whose some seven thousand rules cost the economy $353 billion a year. In 2012, the *Federal Register*, which publishes proposed new rules and final changes to existing rules, comprised 78,961 pages.[63] The Code of Federal Regulations, which publishes general and permanent rules and regulations, totaled 174,545, with over one million individual regulatory restrictions. Just the Dodd-Frank Wall Street Reform and Consumer Protection Act passed in 2010 is up to nearly 14,000 pages of rules—and is only 39 percent complete.[64]

---

61. *Never Enough*, 228.
62. Data at http://www.cbo.gov/sites/default/files/cbofiles/attachments/01-30-Fed
    Pay.pdf.
63. The executive order expanded on the 1969 National Environmental Policy Act, and was reviewed and approved by Congress.
64. Clyde Wayne Crews Jr., "The Ten Thousand Commandments," http://cei.org
    /studies/ten-thousand-commandments-2013.

The Competitive Enterprise Institute puts the annual cost of complying with all these rules and regulations written by anonymous, unaccountable federal bureaucrats at $1.8 trillion.[65] The costs of such extensive regulation obviously reduce economic freedom and thus impair economic growth. Just since 2000, the United States has slipped from being ranked second in freedom from regulation to seventeenth in 2013, according to the Cato Institute.[66] The Heritage Foundation reports that between 2008 and 2013, the United States' overall economic freedom ranking went from sixth to twelfth.[67] But government regulatory intrusion also insidiously compromises the freedom of people and businesses to an extent undreamed of by an ancient tyrant armed only with physical force.

This corrosion of freedom and autonomy is made politically palatable by the redistribution of income to large numbers of people. The federal government spends billions of dollars on thousands of programs every year, but the biggest expense by far is on entitlement spending, which along with the interest on the debt necessary to afford such outlays consumes one-seventh of the economy. In 2012, Medicare, Medicaid, Social Security, and other health spending made up 45 percent of the $3.6 trillion budget, with another 19 percent going to federal employee retirement and benefits, veterans' benefits, and antipoverty programs such as food stamps and welfare.[68] Just the more than eighty programs targeting the poor (including Medicaid) cost nearly $916 billion in 2012.[69]

As well as cost, the range of beneficiaries of such programs has expanded. And as the history of Social Security demonstrates, these programs over time always expand benefits and the number of recipi-

---

65. Crews, "The Ten Thousand Commandments." For Dodd-Frank, see http://www.davispolkportal.com/infographic/july2013infographic.html.
66. Cato Institute, "Economic Freedom of the World," http://www.cato.org/economic-freedom-world.
67. Amy Payne, "This Is Not a Ranking We Should Be Proud Of," http://blog.heritage.org/2014/01/14/economic-freedom-u-s-dropping-rankings.
68. Data at: http://www.heritage.org/research/reports/2013/08/federal-spending-by-the-numbers-2013.
69. Robert Rector, "How the War on Poverty Was Lost," *Wall Street Journal* (January 8, 2014), http://online.wsj.com/news/articles/SB10001424052702303345104579282760272285556?mod=WSJ_Opinion_LEADTop.

ents through the liberalization of eligibility requirements. For example, as a result of the loosening of medical eligibility criteria in the Social Security Disability Benefits Reform Act of 1984, the number of workers receiving Social Security Disability Insurance increased from 2.9 million in 1980 to 10.9 million in 2012, at a cost of $137 billion. This trend will leave the program insolvent in 2016.[70] Likewise the Supplemental Nutritional Aid Program, once known as food stamps, has followed the pattern of expansion set by the Social Security Programs. Over the last decade the number of people receiving food stamps has more than doubled to 47.6 million, but the cost of benefits has quadrupled to $80.4 billion in 2012.[71] Among able-bodied adults without dependents, between fiscal year 2007 and 2010 participation in the program doubled, from 1.7 million to 3.9 million.[72] As a result of this expansive network of government transfers, today about half of all households in the United States receive some sort of federal benefit.[73]

Given the tidal wave of 76 million Baby Boomer retirements that began in 2011 and continues at the rate of ten thousand a day, in addition to the tendency of entitlement programs to expand the number of beneficiaries and the amount of benefits, entitlement costs are projected to increase steeply over the next ten years, as will the federal debt necessary

---

70. See http://www.frbsf.org/economic-research/publications/economic-letter/2013 /june/future-social-security-disability-insurance-ssdi; and http://online.wsj.com /news/articles/SB10001424052702304753504579282293690041708?mod =WSJ_hps_LEFTTopStories.
71. CBO, "Overview of Supplemental Nutrition Assistance Program," http://www .cbo.gov/publication/43175.
72. Rachel Sheffield, "Guess What Group Is Getting Food Stamps at an Alarming Rate," http://blog.heritage.org/2014/01/16/guess-group-getting-food-stamps -alarming-rate.
73. Census Bureau, http://www.census.gov/sipp/tables/quarterly-est/household-char /hsehld-char-11.html. Through payroll taxes workers do contribute to Social Security and Medicare benefits, but not nearly enough to cover the total costs. Most people at all income levels on average will receive two to five times more in benefits from both programs than they paid in, depending on income and family size. See Philip Moeller, "The Best Life," *US News and World Report* (July 1, 2011), http://money.usnews.com/money/blogs/the-best-life/2011/07/01/seniors -dont-pay-full-medicare-social-security-share.

to fund these programs—Social Security and other health care programs costs are projected to double to $3 trillion in the next decade, and debt interest costs to increase nearly three-and-a-half times to $823 billion. But if interest rates return to the average of the '90s, that cost will increase by another $1.4 trillion.[74] The total amount of unfunded liabilities for Social Security and health care entitlements is conservatively estimated to be $123 trillion, and could be as high as $200 trillion.[75]

The bulk of the funds for all this government largesse, of course, comes from federal income taxes, which are designed to redistribute money from the better off to the less well off. In fact, the United States has one of the most progressive tax systems in the world; as of 2008 it was *the* most progressive of the twenty-four richest countries, according to the Organization of Economic Cooperation and Development. That year the top 10 percent in the United States accounted for 45.1 percent of taxes, but earned 33.5 percent of income, a ratio of taxes to income that is higher than European states with more generous social welfare transfers like Germany (31.2/29.2) or Sweden (26.7/26.6).[76] In 2010, the top 40 percent paid 106.2 percent of income taxes, while the bottom 40 percent paid a *negative* 9.1 percent, according to the Congressional Budget Office, due to programs such as the Earned Income Tax Credit and the child tax credit.[77]

This progressivity of US income taxes results in a redistribution of wealth from higher-income to lower-income citizens, even taking into account payroll and state taxes. According to the Tax Foundation, "The

---

74. For these data see compilation of Congressional Budget Office Data at http:// www.heritage.org/research/reports/2013/08/federal-spending-by-the-numbers -2013.
75. USA Debt Clock, http://www.usadebtclock.com; $200 trillion: Niall Ferguson, *The Great Degeneration* (New York, 2012), 42.
76. OECD, "Alternative Measures of Progressivity of Taxes," http://www.keepeek .com/Digital-Asset-Management/oecd/social-issues-migration-health/growing -unequal_9789264044197-en#page109. European countries acquire additional income to finance their welfare transfers from regressive taxes such as the Value Added Tax, a tax on consumption that hits all income groups.
77. See CBO, *The Distribution of Household Income and Federal Taxes*, http://www .cbo.gov/sites/default/files/cbofiles/attachments/44604-AverageTaxRates.pdf.

typical family in the lowest 20 percent in 2012 (with market incomes between $0 and $17,104) pays an average of $6,331 in total taxes and receives $33,402 in spending from all levels of government. Thus the average amount of redistribution to a typical family in the bottom quintile is estimated to be $27,071. The vast majority of this net benefit, a total of $21,158, comes as a result of federal policies." The top 20 percent, on the other hand, paid $87,076 more in taxes than it received in government spending, while the top 1 percent paid $867,473 in taxes and received $55,078 in spending. In 2012, about $2 trillion was distributed from the top 40 percent to the bottom 60 percent of taxpayers.[78]

The income tax, however, is not the only way the federal government redistributes income. The unfunded liabilities of Social Security and Medicare, and the debt necessary to fund today's entitlement costs, go far beyond the redistribution of property from the rich to the poor about which ancient critics of democracy warned. In addition to that sort of redistribution by our federal income tax, today our government retirement and health care programs also redistribute income from the working young to the retired old through the payroll taxes paid by the young to finance Social Security and Medicare. And Obamacare will do the same by forcing the young to buy more-expensive health care in order to subsidize the older and sicker. Worse yet, our $17 trillion debt, destined to grow in order to fund entitlements, is a redistribution of income from generations not yet born to those living today.

The concentrated size and coercive powers of the federal government, along with its massive redistribution of property from the better off, the young, and the unborn, go far beyond the democratic tyranny prophesized by ancient critics and many founders alike in compromising the freedom of the people. Yet developments peculiar to modernity have been necessary to create what Tocqueville called the "softer despotism."

---

78. Gerald Prante and Scott Hodge, Tax Foundation, "The Distribution of Tax and Spending Policies in the United States," http://taxfoundation.org/article/distribution-tax-and-spending-policies-united-states.

Democracy's Flaws and Modernity

Just as the modern world has expanded the mechanisms for redistributing property, so too the other flaws identified by ancient and modern critics have not just persisted into today's world, but in some cases been magnified by technological and other changes.

The Lack of Knowledge among the Masses

The perennial charge against mass participation in governing—that, as the Old Oligarch said, "Among the common people [is] the greatest ignorance"—continues to be a problem today. As law professor Ilya Somin writes, "The sheer depth of most individual voters' ignorance may be shocking" to the layman unfamiliar with formal research on the topic.[79] Polling data of voters compiled during the 2010 midterm election on a range of issues and policies both domestic and foreign, for example, revealed that a majority of voters knew the correct answers to only three of thirteen questions. During the 2012 presidential election, only 43 percent of the US population had ever heard of the eventual Republican vice-presidential nominee Paul Ryan, and only 32 percent knew that he was a member of the House of Representatives. Often the public approved of contradictory policies. Sixty-five percent approved of President Obama's plan to raise tax rates on those earning more than $250,000 a year, yet 75 percent pegged 30 percent, the rate existing at the time, as the highest rate top earners should pay. As Somin points out about his many other examples, "voters are ignorant not just about specific policy issues but about the structure of government and how it operates," as well as "such basic aspects of the US political system as who has the power to declare war, the respective functions of the three branches of government, and who controls monetary policy."[80] This level of ignorance has remained relatively stable since the 1930s, despite higher levels of education and new technologies for the mass distribution of information.

---

79. In *Democracy and Political Ignorance* (Stanford, 2013), 17.
80. Somin, 22, 17–19.

This political ignorance means that on Election Day voters will often privilege their private interests over the longer-term interests of the country as a whole, just as critics of democracy have argued for twenty-five hundred years. The expansion of entitlement spending reflects this tendency. Polls consistently record a strong anti-big-government sentiment among voters. In 2012, exit polls found that 51 percent of voters thought government "is doing too much." Yet in a 2011 survey large majorities also opposed reductions in Medicare and Social Security spending, the most costly big-government entitlements.[81] In December 2013, 71 percent of the US population considered big government to be the "biggest threat to the US in the future," yet a few months earlier 77 percent had disapproved of House Republicans for attempting to shrink the federal government by slowing down spending and reducing deficits.[82] This incoherence reflects the successful marketing of entitlement programs as "rights," or "earned" by employee contributions.

Finally, the traditional concerns with voter ignorance are amplified by the much larger scope and concentrated power of the federal government, which creates policies and programs of a complexity beyond the ability of most people to understand. Writing about the Social Security program in 1960, economist F. A. Hayek pointed out that "the ordinary economist or sociologist or lawyer is today nearly as ignorant [as the layman] of the details of that complex and ever changing system." If the average voter cannot understand the intricacies of just one program, how can he evaluate the numerous others whose growth has led to more coercive state power and to ever escalating costs? Only the champions and managers of such programs, Hayek continues, will be deemed "experts" to whom the average citizen's judgment must defer, and such "experts" are "almost by definition, persons who are in favor of the principles underlying the policy." Citizen autonomy is ceded to the self-interests of unelected, unaccountable functionaries.[83]

---

81. Somin, 197.

82. http://www.gallup.com/poll/166535/record-high-say-big-government-greatest
-threat.aspx; http://www.washingtonpost.com/page/2010-2019/WashingtonPost
/2013/10/22/National-Politics/Polling/release_272.xml.

83. In *The Constitution of Liberty*, 412.

Demagoguery 2.0

Ignorant of the information necessary to make political decisions that benefit the whole citizenry in the long term, the voters will make political choices that serve their own particular short-term interests and passions. This dynamic leaves them vulnerable to the "worthless demagogues," as Aristotle called them, the political leaders who manipulate the tricks of rhetoric in order to appeal to the selfish interests and irrational passions of the electorate.

The new mass media technologies have obviously increased exponentially the modes and mechanisms of manipulative political communication. As early as the founding era, newspapers and pamphlets were considered tools of political demagoguery. Fisher Ames in 1805 complained that "by supplying an endless stimulus to their [the people's] imagination and passions, [the press] has rendered their temper and habits infinitely worse. . . . Public affairs are transacted now on a stage where all the interests and passions grow out of fiction, or are inspired by the art, and often controlled at the pleasure of the actors."[84] In 1920, Walter Lippmann also decried the baleful influence that mass-circulated newspapers had on politics, particularly the sacrifice of truth, fact, and coherent argument to the ideological preferences of editors and reporters, whose professions had "become confused with the work of preachers, revivalists, prophets and agitators."[85]

Since Lippmann's day mass communication technology has made these dangers even more widespread and destructive. Radio, network television, cable and satellite television news shows, and the Internet—Facebook, blogs, chat rooms, Twitter, online magazines and newspapers—have progressively increased the reach of political speech far beyond the few thousand members of the Athenian Assembly before whom an ancient orator spoke. More pernicious, the mass production and circulation of photographs, film, and videos have put into the hands of modern demagogues a mechanism—the image—that more directly, immediately, and intensely exploits the fears, emotions, and passions of the people,

---

84. "The Dangers of American Liberty," in *The Works of Fisher Ames*, 357.
85. *Liberty and the News* (New York, 1920), 8.

bypassing completely even the modicum of thought necessary for understanding verbal or written communications.

Modern electoral history is filled with examples of the impact of an image on the fortunes of a campaign. The September 1960 televised debate between Richard Nixon and John F. Kennedy—Nixon appearing pale, underweight from a recent illness, and sweaty, while Kennedy looked youthful, vigorous, and confident—is universally acknowledged as the event that changed political campaigns forever. Since televised debates between candidates for every political office are these days ubiquitous, now the subjective or irrational perceptions of a politician's appearance, duplicitous rhetoric, and demeanor are more important than his ability to communicate a sound argument, respond cogently to his opponent's ideas, or articulate clearly his principles. A genuine debate is difficult in any case in modern political debates between candidates, which are an exchange of little more than sound bites, with scant time allowed for the candidate to develop a complex thought or critique specifically his opponent's arguments.

Television has also become the medium of political advertisements that manipulate emotionally powerful images in order to demonize an opponent and distort his record or opinions. The foundational example occurred in the 1964 presidential contest between Republican Barry Goldwater and Lyndon Johnson. In order to paint Goldwater as an extremist who could not be trusted with control of nuclear weapons, the Johnson campaign televised an ad in which a winsome girl picking the petals off a daisy disappears into a mushroom cloud. In the 1988 presidential campaign between George H. W. Bush and Massachusetts governor Michael Dukakis, Republicans ran an ad featuring a sinister-looking black felon named Willy Horton, who on a weekend furlough from a Massachusetts prison had raped and assaulted a woman in Maryland. The governor of Massachusetts at the time was Dukakis, who was branded as being soft on crime. More recently, Congressman Paul Ryan, the Republican candidate for vice-president in 2012 whose proposed budget had called for modest entitlement reform, was depicted in an attack ad pushing a granny in a wheelchair over a cliff. The image successfully demonized Ryan and the Republicans as heartless and indifferent to the poor and old. Like televised debates, such ads are now one of the most important modes of communication for both parties.

Finally, the volume of communication both verbal and visual now is huge, the turnover of new commentary and images measured in seconds, and their reach via cell-phone cameras minutely intrusive and immediate. This vast apparatus for rapidly generating 24/7 new information, opinion, and images confuses fact with fiction, reducing political communication to a form of marketing, or of entertainment that gratifies at the same time it reinforces and manipulates the political ideologies of the consumers. Now we are slaves not just to the ear, as Thucydides's Cleon complained of his fellow Athenians, but to the eye as well.

Accountability of Politicians to the People

The overweening power of the tyrant does not free him from accountability. As Plato suggested, he must continue to buy the support of the people, or risk losing his power. On the one hand, the vaster scale of US democracy would suggest that modern politicians are less accountable than were those of ancient Athens, a small town in which leaders could be confronted personally in the market and other public spaces, and where intrusive formal procedures of accountability and political trials were common. In early America as well, citizens had opportunities for confronting elected officials face to face. Yet technology has provided the modern voter novel means of applying electoral pressure on their representatives, and punishing those who threaten their interests.

Of course, politicians still have to be elected, and voters who perceive their interests have been neglected can hold politicians accountable on election day. The United States' electoral history is full of representatives, senators, and presidents thrown out of power by disgruntled voters, despite the advantages of incumbency and contributions from special interest lobbies. In the 2010 midterm elections, voters concerned with sluggish economic growth, the Affordable Care Act, and tax rates—all issues that threatened their economic interests—voted sixty-three Democrats out of the House of Representatives, giving control of the House to Republicans in the largest change of seats since 1948. But high-tech forms of accountability have arisen that increase the scope and intensity of voter disapproval or anger beyond the voting booth.

The new media discussed above obviously can be used to express voters' feelings and opinions almost minute by minute. An ancient Athenian office-holder might be accosted in the agora by a disgruntled citizen for a few minutes, or pilloried on the comic stage for a few hours, but he never was bombarded 24/7 with the incessant opinions and comments filling the millions of blogs, chat rooms, and online magazines, not to mention the attendant sometimes crude and vicious comments. Moreover, much of this commentary is unrestrained by any protocols of decorum, civility, logic, or even truth, with rumors and false charges sharing virtual space with factual information and more serious arguments. Photographs and videos, now instantaneously, and sometimes secretly, recorded on billions of cellular phones, can record a politician's every foible, gaffe, slip of the tongue, or embarrassing faux pas and circulate it to millions of viewers through online sites like YouTube.

The resulting damage to a candidate's or an office-holder's public reputation can end his career or damage his effectiveness. The anxiety over such public opinion can function as a form of preemptive accountability, as few flawed humans can survive having their lives and words scrutinized so minutely, or be routinely subjected to the irrational, malevolent, or subjective judgments of millions of strangers. Hence political action and speech will be relentlessly subjected not to principle or truth, but to the calculus of possible blowback from social media and Internet sites.

Another modern mechanism for applying pressure on elected officials is the public opinion survey and the whole panoply of political polling that surrounds campaigns and elections. Over the last fifty years these polls have proliferated, and today more than fifty polling organizations, polls conducted by print and television media, and numerous other commissioned polls generate daily surveys of opinion. To its champions, polling is a manifestation of democracy and equal representation, a way for the mass of people to exert influence and pressure on their elected officials, and for media to scrutinize the claims of support for policies politicians often make.

For the antidemocrat, however, the assumption that mass public opinion, gleaned from subjective answers to loaded questions, should be considered of equal value to factual knowledge or greater wisdom, and thus can form the basis of political action, is dangerous. As we saw in Chapter 1, Socrates made the reliance on the uninformed, self-interested, or irrational opinions of the mass citizenry the fatal flaw of Athenian democracy. In his day the orators in the Assembly and the comic poets were the purveyors and validators of these shifting and irrational opinions. Today constant polling and surveys, their results instantly and widely disseminated through mass media, have magnified the power of opinion far beyond anything Socrates could have imagined. These data from polls and surveys, moreover, consistently determine the political decisions Congress and the president make, and so serve as councilors to government that bypass the constitutional machinery of checks and balances. As political philosopher Robert Weissberg writes, "The national sample stealthily surmounts the firewalls of decentralized federalism. Constitutional designs impeding public outbursts (e.g., calendar fixed elections, supermajorities) are now rendered obsolete by the majoritarian 'morning after' survey. . . . The once feared, excited *vox populi* now provides wise counsel," and "unveiled, distorted appetites are then artfully raised up to legitimate democratic instructions."[86]

This intense subjection of politicians to voter displeasure or even whim has made it difficult, if not impossible, to reform the entitlement programs whose costs are the drivers of increasing debt and deficits. As *New York Times* columnist David Brooks writes, "Many voters have decided they like spending a lot on themselves and pushing costs onto their children and grandchildren. They have decided they like borrowing up to $1 trillion a year for tax credits, disability payments, defense contracts and the rest. They have found that the original Keynesian rationale for these deficits provides a perfect cover for permanent

---

86. *Polling, Policy, and Public Opinion* (New York, 2002), 4, 5.

deficit-living. They have made it clear that they will destroy any politician who tries to stop them from cost-shifting in this way."[87]

Radical Egalitarianism

The ancient critics of democracy warned against the degeneration of equality of opportunity and equality under the law into radical egalitarianism, which as Aristotle said, "arises out of the notion that those who are equal in any respect are equal in all respects; because men are equally free, they claim to be absolutely equal."[88] In 1835 Tocqueville recognized this same tendency in the United States. He contrasted the "manly and lawful passion for equality" that spurred men to advance their station, with a "depraved taste for equality, which impels the weak to attempt to lower the powerful to their own level."[89] This sort of equality necessarily demands equality of result, no matter how deficient anyone is in talent, ability, brains, industry, or even luck. The founding generation fretted constantly over what they called a "leveling spirit," the desire for absolute equality and the destruction of distinctions of talent and achievement among citizens that give the lie to radical egalitarianism.

This "leveling spirit," moreover, was the dynamic for redistributing property, as differences of wealth are the daily, concrete reminder of those distinctions. As Madison wrote in *The Federalist* 10, "From the protection of different and unequal faculties of acquiring property, the possession of different degrees and kinds of property immediately results: and from the influence of these on the sentiments and views of the respective proprietors, ensues a division of the society into different interests and parties."[90] Hence the Progressive focus on class distinctions and "fiscal justice" as great evils to be remedied by the federal gov-

---

87. "Another Fiscal Flop," January 1, 2013, http://www.nytimes.com/2013/01/01 /opinion/brooks-another-fiscal-flop.html?n=Top%2fOpinion%2fEditorials %20and%20Op%2dEd%2fOp%2dEd%2fColumnists%2fDavid%20Brooks &_r=0.
88. *Politics* 1301a, trans. Jowett.
89. *Democracy in America*, vol. 1, 53; see also 201.
90. Madison 10, 44.

ernment, for they perpetuate the "different interests and parties" that impair the national unity Progressives believed to be necessary for the country's well-being and achievement of "social justice."

Equalization of wealth through redistributive policies continues to be a major expression of radical egalitarianism. "Income inequality," for example, is routinely decried as a great injustice, as happened in December 2013 when President Obama condemned "a dangerous and growing inequality and lack of upward mobility."[91] Yet in today's United States, this concern is a dubious cliché of class-warfare rhetoric. In fact, when the value of government transfers such as Medicaid and the Earned Income Tax Credit are included in calculating income, income inequality actually declined 1.8 percent between 1993 and 2009.[92] But the class-warfare rhetoric of "income inequality" justifies the redistributionist and entitlement policies that in turn require an expanded federal government and its intrusive powers.

The Progressive expansion of "rights," however, such as the "right" to a more equitable income, was accompanied by an expansion of equality to include not just wealth, but the satisfaction of subjective "needs." Frank Giddings, a sociologist at Columbia University, specified these "equal needs" in his 1898 book *Democracy and Social Organization*: "opportunity for expansion and development of life," "human sympathy and companionship," and "emancipation from fear," all of which Giddings posited as comprising the "fundamental demand of democracy" that must be satisfied by the government. Other "modes of equality" that Giddings claimed "must be sedulously maintained in a democratic community" included "equality of sanitary conditions," "certain means of recreation and culture," "fair play," "courtesy," and "regard for certain fundamental social values" such as "respect for expert knowledge." This utopian laundry list of psychic goods once thought the consequence of individual talent, hard work, inclination, virtue, or luck can be realized

---

91. Politico, "President Obama on Inequality," http://www.politico.com/story/2013/12/obama-income-inequality-100662.html.

92. Kip Hagopian and Lee Ohanian, "The Mismeasure of Inequality," *Policy Review* (August 2012), http://www.hoover.org/publications/policy-review/article/123566.

only by a coercive governmental power intruding into social and economic life to compensate for the unequal distribution of those advantages and resources among the citizens.[93]

We have progressed far beyond Giddings's expansive definition of equality. As political philosopher Kenneth Minogue points out, today "almost any kind of inequality counts as oppression," making "a fully democratic society as one that makes available to each of its members the full panoply of benefits in, and appropriate to, a modern society. They range from material things on the one hand to respect and attention on the other."[94] Political and social institutions must now validate subjective perceptions of the esteem people feel they deserve, something even the egalitarian Athenians only entertained in the fantasies of comedies like Aristophanes' *Women at Assembly*, in which laws are passed that compel the attractive young to become the sexual partners of the homely old.

This concern with the impact of inequality on the psyches and self-esteem of citizens is something peculiar to the modern world. It is in part a consequence of the unprecedented spread of wealth and improvement in material existence to millions once mired in poverty and deprivation. This success has seemingly repudiated the tragic view of a flawed human nature limited by a world filled with want, scarcity, and risk, a world in which the only equality is that of everyone's vulnerability to all these contingencies. For us, on the contrary, since the technological means have been created to mitigate physical wants and provide material goods to more and more people, we believe that knowledge and techniques must exist for creating an equality of psychic well-being as well, if only the unjust economic, political, and social structures that presumably create this unhappiness and disrespect can be improved.

And just as inequality of property is a problem for a powerful federal government to correct by redistributing property, so too coercive laws and regulations are created to eliminate or improve whatever unjust social and economic structures damage the self-esteem and happiness of citizens, and to punish those complicit in perpetuating inequality, par-

---

93. In Eisenach, 92–93.
94. *The Servile Mind* (New York, 2010), 37.

ticularly for those deemed victims of previous social or political oppression. This coercive power, Minogue writes, reduces the individual's autonomy and creates the "structural conditions of the servile mind," including "the legal and regulatory structures designed to protect one or other abstract category in the community from being harassed, offended, damaged in self-esteem, or made to suffer many other things officially construed as oppressive."[95] Hate speech regulations and sexual harassment laws, which frequently abridge the First Amendment right to free speech, are examples of the coercive power of the state directed toward elevating the esteem and psychic well-being of selected groups at the expense of others. Just as the antidemocratic tradition predicts, the masses who turn to a centralized power to bestow equality end up finding it in their equal subjection to a tyrant. As Tocqueville said, radical egalitarianism "reduces men to prefer equality in slavery to inequality with freedom."[96]

Freedom Degenerates into License

Ancient critics of democracy agreed that political freedom was not the ability to live as one likes—indulging every transient desire or gratifying every appetite—but to live subject to the limits of law both written and unwritten, the only life suitable for a rational and virtuous human being. Thus a state designed for political freedom should aim to achieve moral "excellence," as Aristotle writes, and "to make the citizens good and just."[97] Democracy, on the other hand, by empowering the many despite their lack of virtue or wisdom, will create citizens who, as Plato says, call "anarchy liberty" and give themselves over to "the freedom and libertinism of useless and unnecessary pleasures."[98] The founding generation agreed, continually fretting over the degeneration of democracy into license and ultimately tyranny. "The known propensity of a democracy," Fisher Ames wrote, "is to licentiousness, which the ambi-

---

95. *The Servile Mind*, 6.
96. *Democracy in America*, vol. 1, 53.
97. *Politics* 1280b, trans. Jowett.
98. *Republic* 560e–61c, trans. Jowett.

tious call, and the ignorant believe to be, liberty." For, as Ames continues, "The individual who is left to act according to his own humor is not governed at all; and if any considerable number, and especially any combination of individuals, find or can place themselves in this situation, then the society is no longer free. For liberty obviously consists in the salutary restraint, and not in the uncontrolled indulgence of such humors."[99]

In the United States today, ordered liberty has indeed been reduced for many to mere license, as the ancients predicted and the founders feared. Two developments of modernity have contributed to this process. The first has been secularization, the driving of religion from the public square and the reduction of it to a private lifestyle choice no more significant than any other. In contrast, the Founders were united in believing that political order and freedom for the many depended on the transcendent sanctions of religion to restrain the fallen nature of people and their destructive appetites. George Washington's remarks in his 1796 Farewell Address express this widespread belief: "Of all the dispositions and habits which lead to political prosperity, religion and morality are indispensable supports," the "firmest props of the duties of men and citizens. . . . Whatever may be conceded to the influence of refined education on minds of peculiar structure, reason and experience both forbid us to expect that national morality can prevail in exclusion of religious principle."[100] Only through religious faith can the moral order created by "Nature's God" and the "Supreme Judge of the world," as the Declaration of Independence put it, marginalize license and appetitive self-indulgence, and minimize its power to sanction destructive behavior. Without these internal restraints, only the all-powerful state, managed by flawed humans susceptible to the corruption of power, will be the authority for regulating people's lives and behavior, one subject not to transcendent morality and disinterested principle, but to the political preferences and interests of those in power.

———————

99. "The Dangers of American Liberty," 349, 359.
100. George Washington's Farewell Address, http://avalon.law.yale.edu/18th _century/washing.asp.

The erosion of religious authority has facilitated the other development of modernity that changes ordered liberty into license—the "sexual revolution." The managers of the Leviathan state have understood that sexuality is the most effective appetite to exploit in order to distract people from their loss of political autonomy and independence. The consequences of the sexual revolution—cheap contraception, destruction of sexual taboos, widely available pornography, the sexualization of popular culture and the Public Square, and at-will abortion—have legitimized sexual indulgence and helped to erode the classical political virtues of self-control and restraint. At the same time, by separating sex from procreation, sexual license has weakened the family as an intermediary authority between the individual and the state, which has encouraged this license with government-funded birth control and abortions, and with public school curricula that legitimize and encourage it. Sexual freedom—which is in fact what the ancients would have called the enslavement of the mind to the body's pleasures—has now replaced political freedom and autonomy as the highest expression of liberty.

All these novel developments of the modern world that magnify the traditional dangers of democracy are mutually reinforcing, and together work to empower the Leviathan state and insidiously erode the freedom and autonomy of citizens. James Kalb has expressed well this nexus inherent in the "managerial liberal regime": "What defines that regime is the effort to manage and rationalize social life in order to bring it in line with comprehensive standards aimed at implementing equal freedom. The result is a pattern of governance intended to promote equality and individual gratification and marked by entitlement programs, sexual and expressive freedoms, blurred distinctions between the public and the private, and the disappearance of self-government."[101] As Plato predicted, "drunk on the wine of freedom," the citizens will sacrifice ordered liberty and personal responsibility as long as the state subsidizes their licentious self-indulgence with wealth transfers through entitlement programs.

---

101. *The Tyranny of Liberalism* (Wilmington, DE, 2008), 5–6.

The Dangers of Modern Democratic Foreign Policy

The substitution of verbal deliberation and procedure for coercion is the glory of constitutional governments. Yet as the history of ancient Athens shows, verbal processes of decision-making can be dangerous for foreign policy. Deliberation and diplomacy too often become excuses for avoiding military force when citizens and politicians do not want to pay the costs in lives and money required for timely action. The frequent election cycles and accountability of policy-makers to voters typical of democracy also make the long-range planning vital for foreign policy difficult. In 1835 Tocqueville recognized these dangers, remarking that a "clear perception of the future, founded upon judgment and experience . . . is frequently wanting in democracies. The people are more apt to feel than to reason; and if their present sufferings are great, it is to be feared that the still greater sufferings attendant upon defeat will be forgotten." Particularly in foreign affairs, "a democracy can only with great difficulty regulate the details of an important undertaking, persevere in a fixed design, and work out its execution in spite of serious obstacles. It cannot combine its measures with secrecy or await their consequences with patience."[102] Winston Churchill agreed, attributing the slaughter of World War II partly to "the structure and habits of democratic states," which "lack those elements of persistence and conviction which can alone give security to the humble masses," and in which "even in matters of self-preservation, no policy is pursued for even ten or fifteen years at a time."[103]

The United States' foreign policy over the last decade under both political parties has illustrated these weaknesses. The resort to diplomatic engagement to provide cover for inaction is most obvious in the failure to keep North Korea from obtaining nuclear weapons. Three decades of talks, UN resolutions, International Atomic Energy Agency inspections, interim agreements, "agreed frameworks," sanctions, and "moratoriums" ended up with a rogue state in possession of nuclear weapons. Despite

---

102. *Democracy in America*, 1.13.
103. *The Second World War*, vol. 1, *The Gathering Storm* (1948; New York, 1985), 16.

that failure, the same scenario is unfolding with regard to Iran's nuclear weapons program. In November 2013, President Obama announced that Iran had agreed to talk again in six months, in exchange for the West's loosening of some economic sanctions and Iran's promises merely to slow down enrichment—negating seven UN Security Council resolutions that it must halt enrichment—and to admit inspectors. This sort of futile diplomatic engagement functions as political cover for the administration and much of the US population, who are unwilling to risk military force to compel Iran to abandon its weapons program. Meanwhile Iran, like North Korea before it, can manipulate the diplomatic process to buy time for reaching its goal of a nuclear weapon, with serious consequences for the United States' security and interests.

Similarly, the withdrawal of US troops from Iraq at the end of 2011, without a status-of-forces agreement sanctioning a US military presence, reflected the war-weariness of many politicians and US citizens, despite the risk that a precipitate withdrawal would squander the lives and money expended over the previous decade in order to eliminate Iraq as a threat to the United States' interests. So too with the announced withdrawal from Afghanistan by the end of 2014. As Tocqueville warned, the short-term benefits of ending the expenditure of money and lives take precedence over the long-term dangers that the gains made against the Taliban will be wasted, and a terrorist organization hostile to our security and interests will once more find safe harbor, the very danger the war was fought to avoid.

As in ancient Athens, these shortsighted decisions in part reflect the desire to spend money on social welfare entitlements rather than on defense. The irony is that the cost of the wars in Afghanistan and Iraq over eleven years, $1.4 trillion, was only 4 percent of federal spending, and nine-tenths of 1 percent of the $163 trillion the economy produced during that same period.[104] Yet spending any amount of money on butter

---

104. Robert Samuelson, "Syria and the myth that Americans are 'war weary,'" *Washington Post*, September 4, 2013, http://www.washingtonpost.com/opinions /robert-samuelson-syria-and-the-war-weary-myth/2013/09/04/cb03c268 -1566-11e3-a2ec-b47e45e6f8ef_story.html.

rather than guns is frequently the favorite option for democracies in which federal transfers benefit so many citizens. Thus the "sequester" cuts mandated by the 2011 Budget Control Act called for half a trillion dollars in defense cuts over the next decade, half the amount of all reductions, while the main drivers of the deficit, Social Security, Medicare, and Medicaid, were left untouched. Just as the ancient Athenians in the fourth century BC preferred to spend money on state pay for themselves rather than on defense, many citizens today seem concerned less with preparing for the future threats to the United States' security and interest, than with ensuring that entitlement spending continues.

In addition to these traditional weaknesses of democratic foreign policy, modernity has added another, idealistic democracy promotion, something unknown to the Athenian democracy, which promoted democratic government in other city-states, often by the sword, in order to defend Athens's economic and imperial interests. Today democracy promotion reflects an idealistic internationalism based not on a balance of power codified in treaties that mutually serve the interests of sovereign nations, but on an ideal of progress beyond war to a world unified in its pacific beliefs and aims. Assuming that all peoples everywhere desire the same goods as Westerners—especially economic development, political freedom, human rights, and peace—this ideal looks to transnational organizations and international treaties to adjudicate conflict through verbal processes and negotiations, and to promote the creation of liberal democracy and free-market economies in order to bestow freedom and prosperity on those lacking them. One of the early international treaties embodying this ideal, the First Hague Conventions, set out these goals in 1899: "the maintenance of the general peace" through "the friendly settlement of international disputes," based on the "solidarity which unites the members of the society of civilized nations" and their desire for "extending the empire of law, and of strengthening the appreciation of international justice."[105]

---

105. Text of the First Hague Convention, http://avalon.law.yale.edu/19th_century /hague01.asp. The following paragraphs adapted from my article "Obama's

This foreign policy idealism has attracted presidents from both parties for nearly a century. The Progressive Woodrow Wilson found it congenial, basing the entry of the United States into World War I in part on the notion that global order depended on the spread of democracy. In his 1917 speech asking Congress for a declaration of war against Germany, Wilson said that the purpose of the war was "to vindicate the principles of peace and justice in the life of the world as against selfish and autocratic power," for "peace can never be maintained except by a partnership of democratic nations." Thus "the world must be made safe for democracy. Its peace must be planted upon the tested foundations of political liberty." The people of the United States "are but one of the champions of the rights of mankind. We shall be satisfied when those rights have been made as secure as the faith and the freedom of nations can make them." Implicit in Wilson's remarks is the idea that freedom, democracy, and peace are the default political goals for the whole world.[106]

After the end of the Cold War with the collapse of the Soviet Union, the Wilsonian dream of using foreign policy to promote democracy was given new life. President George H. W. Bush sounded the Wilsonian note in his 1991 State of the Union address delivered during the first Gulf War against Iraq. The fast-approaching disintegration of the Soviet Union seemingly confirmed the triumph of democracy and the establishment of "a new world order," Bush said, "where diverse nations are drawn together in common cause to achieve the universal aspirations of mankind—peace and security, freedom, and the rule of law." The Gulf War against Saddam Hussein was in part motivated by this idealism, even if more realist goals of protecting Saudi Arabia and its oil reserves were no doubt more important.[107]

Despite the subsequent bloody global conflicts, civil wars, al-Qaeda's terrorist attacks, and the brutal ethnic cleansing in Sudan and the Balkans

---

Foreign Policy Delusions," published October 22, 2012, in *Defining Ideas* (http://www.hoover.org/publications/defining-ideas/article/131041).
106. Woodrow Wilson's War Message to Congress, http://wwi.lib.byu.edu/index .php/Wilson<#213>s_War_Message_to_Congress.
107. George H. W. Bush's State of the Union, http://www.presidency.ucsb.edu/ws /?pid=19253.

that marred the 1990s, the democracy dream maintained it potency. President George W. Bush, in the 2002 National Security Strategy, defined the foreign policy of the United States as promoting a "single sustainable model for national success: freedom, democracy, and free enterprise," for "these values of freedom are right and true for every person, in every society." Thus the United States will strive "to extend the benefits of freedom across the globe. We will actively work to bring the hope of democracy, development, free markets, and free trade to every corner of the world."[108] Bush returned to these themes in January 2005 in his inaugural address, in which he linked US security and global peace to the "force of human freedom" and the expansion of democracy: "The survival of liberty in our land increasingly depends on the success of liberty in other lands. The best hope for peace in our world is the expansion of freedom in all the world."[109] The wars in Afghanistan and Iraq were fought not just to drive out the Taliban and destroy Hussein's regime, but also to create political freedom and democratic institutions.

Barack Obama, though as a senator he was a critic of such "nation-building," as president has at least in his rhetoric endorsed these same goals. As he said on June 4, 2009, in his Cairo speech, "I do have an unyielding belief that all people yearn for certain things: the ability to speak your mind and have a say in how you are governed; confidence in the rule of law and the equal administration of justice; government that is transparent and doesn't steal from the people; the freedom to live as you choose. These are not just American ideas; they are human rights. And that is why we will support them everywhere."[110]

In his September 2012 remarks at the UN, Obama again reprised the tradition of US idealism stretching back to Woodrow Wilson. He endorsed "the notion that people can resolve their differences peace-

---

108. White House, National Security Strategy, http://georgewbush-whitehouse
     .archives.gov/nsc/nss/2002.
109. George W. Bush's Second Inaugural Address, http://avalon.law.yale.edu/21st
     _century/gbush2.asp.
110. "Remarks by the President on a New Beginning," http://www.whitehouse.gov
     /the_press_office/Remarks-by-the-President-at-Cairo-University-6-04-09.

fully; that diplomacy can take the place of war; that in an interdependent world, all of us have a stake in working towards greater opportunity and security for our citizens." He said the United States supported the various Arab Spring revolts because "we recognized our own beliefs in the aspirations of men and women who took to the streets" and "our support for democracy put us on the side of the people." Echoing George W. Bush, Obama asserted, "Freedom and self-determination are not unique to one culture. These are not simply American values or Western values—they are universal values." Obama also endorsed the ability of democracy to change the world: "I am convinced that ultimately government of the people, by the people and for the people is more likely to bring about the stability, prosperity, and individual opportunity that serve as a basis for peace in our world."[111]

Despite this soaring rhetoric, so far the record of democracy promotion over the last twenty years has been dismal. Globally, Freedom House records 122 electoral democracies, yet the number of countries designated as free stands at 88, two fewer than the previous year.[112] The Middle East, the main focus of this country's democracy's promotion over the last decade, illustrates this trend. Iraq is again subjected to terrorist violence at the hands of a reinvigorated al-Qaeda, and the government has grown closer to Iran, the leading state supporter of terrorism and an inveterate enemy of the US. Afghanistan appears increasingly unlikely to ward off a resurgent Taliban once US forces leave. The Arab Spring revolts that many believed to herald democratization in the Muslim Middle East have either empowered Islamist factions, as in Libya and Tunisia; restored illiberal regimes, as in Egypt; or degenerated into brutal civil war, as in Syria. This failure is consistent with other efforts to build democracy in Somalia, South Sudan, Haiti, Bosnia, and Kosovo.[113]

111. "Remarks by the President to the UN General Assembly," http://www.whitehouse.gov/the-press-office/2012/09/25/remarks-president-un-general-assembly.
112. Freedom House, "The Democratic Leadership Gap," http://www.freedomhouse.org/report/overview-fact-sheet#.UuFPHaWtuiy.
113. Michael Mandelbaum, *Democracy's Good Name* (New York, 2007), 90.

This failure reflects the modern naiveté about the conditions required for genuine liberal democracy and political freedom to flourish, since these are, as Michael Mandelbaum points out, "embodied in institutions, which operate through habits and skills and are supported by values. All take time to develop, and they must develop independently and domestically; they cannot be imported ready-made."[114] Moreover, there is no historical evidence that the desire to live as one wants and to participate in governing one's community, hallmarks of democracies, *necessarily* trumps all other goods and aims that humans desire and pursue. People also desire security and protection from danger, including the consequences of their own choices, as much as or at times even more than freedom. They often cherish group loyalty and communal obligations, fealty to their gods and religious doctrines, national, tribal, or ethnic identity and its honor, revenge against enemies, martial glory, conquest and domination of other peoples, or various ideologies more than they prize freedom and prosperity, and often will trade away the latter in order to honor or obtain those other goods.

Different cultures with different histories will not, then, always find the boons of liberal democracy as self-evident or as superior to other goods as we. As diplomat and political philosopher George Kennan in 1977 observed, "I know of no evidence that 'democracy' . . . is the natural state of most of mankind," as it has "a relatively narrow base both in time and in space; and the evidence has yet to be produced that it is the natural form of rule for peoples outside those narrow perimeters. . . . Those Americans who profess to know with such certainty what other people want and what is good for them in the way of political institutions would do well to ask themselves whether they are not actually attempting to impose their own values, traditions, and habits of thoughts on peoples for whom these things have no validity and no usefulness."[115] The dangers of this attitude have been particularly obvious in the failure of the "Arab Spring" revolts, where an obsession with the act of democratic voting—as the Freedom House data above show, something

---

114. *Democracy's Good Name*, 183.
115. *The Cloud of Danger* (Boston, 1977), 42–43.

not necessarily indicative of freedom—as a self-evident good obscured the risk of empowering an illiberal, intolerant political order of the sort that in the event many of the newly liberated people voted for. Elsewhere too, the "one-size-fits-all democratization strategy," as Joshua Kurlantzick calls it, has led to a global retreat from democracy in recent years that threatens dangerous consequences for our national security and interests.[116]

The point is not that all peoples would not in fact eventually prefer to live under a liberal democratic government that gives them freedom and economic opportunity, rules by law rather than arbitrary force, and respects human rights. The patterns of emigration from autocracies and dictatorships to the free, prosperous West suggests otherwise. Rather, what is dangerous is the notion that any country, no matter how militarily powerful or well intentioned, can create democracy, which took twenty-three hundred years to develop in the West, in other countries lacking that long history, without an open-ended commitment of military forces, and an intrusive control over their governments and economies redolent of nineteenth-century imperialism.

The impatience of democracies with even short-term expenditures of lives and money makes such a long-term commitment unlikely, particularly in the United States, with its traditional distrust of Thomas Jefferson's "entangling alliances," imperialism, and military involvement abroad.[117] From its beginnings, as John Quincy Adams famously said in 1821, while a "well-wisher to the freedom and independence of all," America "goes not abroad, in search of monsters to destroy," and has preferred to promote democracy "by the countenance of her voice, and benign sympathy of her example."[118] That preference is still a powerful part of the United States' political DNA.

Yet we live in a world very different from that of John Quincy Adams, when protected by two oceans the United States could more

116. *Democracy in Retreat* (New Haven, CT, and London, 2013), 173.
117. Thomas Jefferson's First Inaugural Address, 1801, http://avalon.law.yale.edu /19th_century/jefinau1.asp.
118. John Quincy Adams's Address to Congress, 1821, http://millercenter.org /president/speeches/detail/3484.

easily stand aloof from disorders and conflicts abroad. Today a foreign policy actively focused on democracy promotion risks not just the failure of that project and its cost in blood and resources, but also that failure in turn fostering an isolationist sentiment such as we have experienced over the last few years. We heard such traces of isolationism in President Obama's call in July 2012 for "some nation-building here at home," and the claim in his Second Inaugural address not that two wars had been won in Iraq and Afghanistan, but that "a decade of war is now ending" even as victory in both countries is still in doubt.[119] These remarks reflect public sentiment. In December 2013, 52 percent of the US population thought the United States "should mind its own business internationally and let other countries get along the best they can on their own," a forty-year low in support for US global leadership.[120] Unfortunately, a globalized economy knit together by trade, mass media, and jet travel, and threatened by various aggressors from illiberal nations to murderous terrorist organizations, requires a global power subject to law and accountability, and founded on respect for human rights and freedom, to maintain the order necessary for that global economy to function. At this point in history, the United States is the only nation possessing those critical virtues and the requisite military and economic power, which make it capable and worthy enough to be trusted with that responsibility. Turning our back on it will create a world more dangerous for our security and interests.

A Kinder, Gentler Leviathan

Speaking before the Virginia constitutional ratifying convention in 1788, James Madison warned, "Since the general civilization of mankind, I believe there are more instances of the abridgment of the free-

---

119. "Obama: Time for Nation-Building at Home," http://www.upi.com/Top _News/US/2012/07/14/Obama-Time-for-nation-building-at-home/UPI -22451342291780; Barack Obama's Second Inaugural, http://www.forbes.com /sites/beltway/2013/01/21/full-text-president-obamas-inaugural-address.
120. Pew survey, http://www.people-press.org/2013/12/03/public-sees-u-s-power -declining-as-support-for-global-engagement-slips.

dom of the people by gradual and silent encroachments of those in power, than by violent and sudden usurpations." Madison made republics an exception to this general rule, for "turbulence, violence, and abuse of power, by the majority trampling on the rights of the minority, have produced factions and commotions, which, in republics, have, more frequently than any other cause, produced despotism."[121]

The modern United States has disproven Madison's exception, which was consistent with the predictions of democracy's degeneration into tyranny made by ancient critics like Plato, Aristotle, and Polybius. Over the last two centuries, the growth of the federal government at the expense of state sovereignty and citizen self-rule, the legal redistribution of property to fund entitlements that sap the virtue and independence of citizens, and the modern variations of the traditional flaws of democracy have created the conditions for Tocqueville's "softer despotism," which has aggrandized power with "gradual and silent encroachments" on the people's freedom and autonomy.

Tocqueville's justly famous 1840 description of democratic despotism is astonishing in its prescience, and an uncanny prediction of the political and social transformation a century of Progressive ideology has wrought in the United States. Such a tyranny, Tocqueville writes, unlike the violent despots of the past "would be more extensive and more mild, it would degrade men without tormenting him." Egalitarianism, license, and atomistic individualism would contribute to this degradation of "an innumerable multitude of men, all equal and alike, incessantly endeavoring to procure the petty and paltry pleasures with which they glut their lives. Each of them, living apart, is as a stranger to the fate of the rest . . . he exists only in himself and for himself alone; and if his kindred still remain to him, he may be said at any rate to have lost his country."[122]

Such a people will submit to being governed by "an immense and tutelary power, which takes upon itself alone to secure their gratifica-

---

121. Virginia Constitutional Ratifying Convention, http://www.constitution.org/rc /rat_va_05.htm.
122. *Democracy in America*, vol. 2, 318.

tions and to watch over their fate," a power "absolute, minute, regular provident, and mild," and one that, like our federal regulatory regime, "covers the surface of society with a network of small complicated rules, minute and uniform, through which the most original minds and the most energetic characters cannot penetrate." And like the Progressive ideal of a state-provided "decent life" and happiness for the people, Tocqueville's mild tyrant seeks "to keep them in perpetual childhood: it is well content that the people should rejoice, provided they think of nothing but rejoicing. For their happiness such a government willingly labors, but it chooses to be the sole agent and the only arbiter of that happiness; it provides for their security, foresees and supplies their necessities, facilitates their pleasures, manages their principal concerns, directs their industry, regulates the descent of property, and subdivides their inheritances: what remains, but to spare them all the care of thinking and all the trouble of living?"[123] Under this regime, the machinery of representative government will not avail to call the citizens back to autonomy and self-rule: "It is indeed difficult to conceive how men who have entirely given up the habit of self-government should succeed in making a proper choice of those by whom they are to be governed; and no one will ever believe that a liberal, wise, and energetic government can spring from the suffrages of a subservient people."[124]

And so the dangers and discontents of democracy catalogued in the 24 centuries of the antidemocratic tradition lead not to the violent tyranny prophesized by the ancients and feared by the Founders, but to the modern big-government, regulatory welfare state, a kinder and gentler Leviathan, but one no less inimical to freedom.

---

123. *Democracy in America*, vol. 2, 318–19.
124. *Democracy in America*, vol. 2, 321.

CONCLUSION

Restoring Limited Government

The danger of modern liberty is that, absorbed in the enjoyment of our private independence, and in the pursuit of our particular interests, we should surrender our right to share in political power too easily. The holders of authority are only too anxious to encourage us to do so. They are so ready to spare us all sort of troubles, except those of obeying and paying! They will say to us: what, in the end, is the aim of your efforts, the motive of your labors, the object of all your hopes? Is it not happiness? Well, leave this happiness to us and we shall give it to you. No, Sirs, we must not leave it to them. No matter how touching such a tender commitment may be, let us ask the authorities to keep within their limits. Let them confine themselves to being just. We shall assume the responsibility of being happy for ourselves.

—Benjamin Constant[1]

Of all tyrannies, a tyranny sincerely exercised for the good of its victims may be the most oppressive. It would be better to live under robber barons than under omnipotent moral busybodies. The robber baron's cruelty may sometimes sleep, his cupidity may at some point be satiated; but those who torment us for our own good will torment us without end for they do so with the approval of their own conscience. They may be more likely to go to Heaven yet at the same time likelier to make a Hell of earth. This very kindness stings with intolerable insult. To be 'cured' against one's will and cured of states which we may not regard as disease is to be put on a level of those who have not

---

1. "The Liberty of Ancients Compared with that of Moderns," 1816, http://www.uark.edu/depts/comminfo/cambridge/ancients.html.

yet reached the age of reason or those who never will; to be classed with infants, imbeciles, and domestic animals.

—C. S. Lewis[2]

Tocqueville's "soft despotism" is still a work in progress, "a *possible* outcome of the democratic adventure," as political philosopher Daniel Mahoney writes, and will in the end result from choice, not destiny.[3] The United States still possesses the resources of our constitutional structure and US character that make possible a return to our foundational ideas of limited government and citizen self-rule.

Despite all the modifications of the constitutional order, US citizens still have the right to vote every two years. Ballot-box accountability has dangers evident from ancient Athens to today, but nonetheless provides an opportunity for people to change course when the encroaching power of the federal government goes too far, as we witnessed in the 2010 midterm elections that gave Republicans control of the House of Representatives. The ongoing problems with the Affordable Care Act—especially people losing their health insurance or seeing premium costs increasing—may bring home to people the costs of empowering a kinder, gentler Leviathan that "provides for their security [and] foresees and supplies their necessities," as Tocqueville wrote, at the price of ever greater interference and control over their lives. The midterm congressional elections in November 2014 appear likely to punish many members of Congress who supported this legislation, and perhaps mark a growing sense among the electorate that the progressive Leviathan has overreached, that the entitlement state is fiscally and morally unsustainable, and that it is now time to start returning to the constitutional ideals of limited government and citizen self-rule.

2. "The Humanitarian Theory of Punishment," 1949; in *God in the Dock* (Grand Rapids, MI, 1970), 292.
3. *The Conservative Foundations of the Liberal Order* (Wilmington, DE, 2010), 18. Emphasis in original.

Citizens have another form of resistance against federal encroachments—"Irish democracy." This idea originated among Irish Republicans in the early twentieth century, who resisted British rule by refusing to cooperate with the authorities in numerous, often trivial ways. Political philosopher James C. Scott defines it as "the silent, dogged resistance, withdrawal, and truculence of millions of ordinary people."[4] An ongoing example is the refusal of young people so far to sign up for the Affordable Care Act, the linchpin of the program, since the healthy young are necessary to finance the sick and old. Millions of the uninsured for whom the program was designed have likewise refused to participate. Fewer than half the 7 million enrollees expected by the end of January 2014 had signed up, and most of those have been older, sicker, and the previously insured. If these trends continue, the Affordable Care Act will be repealed or seriously modified because millions of citizens simply have refused to participate in the program.

Next, for all the erosion of state sovereignty over the last century, state governments still exist and still remain what Supreme Court Justice Louis Brandeis in 1932 called a "laboratory" in which citizens can "try novel social and economic experiments without risk to the rest of the country."[5] In recent years states have gone their own way on numerous issues such as gun control, voter identification laws, same-sex marriage, restrictions on abortion, or legalizing marijuana. As professor of politics John Dina writes, states have several resources for resisting federal power. They can decriminalize some behaviors, refuse to participate in federal programs, and pass their own laws inconsistent with federal law or Supreme Court precedents.[6] Exploiting these powers and lessening tax burdens and regulations on business allow states to become more successful and illustrate the boons that follow from resisting Leviathan. The worsening economic and social problems in

---

4. In *Two Cheers for Anarchism* (Princeton, NJ, 2012), 14.
5. In *New State Ice Co. v. Liebmann* (1932), http://caselaw.lp.findlaw.com/scripts/getcase.pl?navby=CASE&court=US&vol=285&page=262.
6. "How States Talk Back to Washington and Strengthen American Federalism," *Policy Analysis* (December 3, 2013), http://object.cato.org/sites/cato.org/files/pubs/pdf/pa744_web.pdf.

those states, like California and Illinois, which practice the big-government "blue model," as historian Walter Russell Mead dubs it, and the growing success of those like Texas and Florida following the "red model" of more-limited government power over the economy and social life, illustrate how states can offer attractive alternatives to soft despotism, especially if enough citizens vote with their feet and migrate to successful states.[7]

These trends do not mean that we will restore completely the Constitution's vision of limited government, or dismantle completely the entitlement state. But even if we cannot slay Leviathan, we can put it on a diet. We can reenergize at the state level the constitutional federalism that leaves it to citizens and their local and state governments to work out more efficiently than distant, unaccountable technocrats can the issues most important to them and the solutions more cognizant of their variety of passions and interests. And by doing so we will restore a more robust freedom for all people whatever their political persuasion, for they will be free to leave a state whose policies they dislike and live in another.

Another strength of the United States that offers the possibility of resistance is our civil society, the 1.5 million nonprofit organizations, fraternal societies, and other voluntary associations independent of government in which people can pursue common interests, lobby government, and hold politicians and government agencies accountable.[8] In addition there are 350,000 churches that also can provide alternatives and mobilize resistance to big government, as the Catholic Church has been doing in fighting back against the Affordable Care Act's mandate to provide birth control and abortifacients in health care programs offered by the church.[9] Participation in such organizations, as political philosopher Robert D. Putnam has documented, has declined from

---

7. In "The Once and Future Liberalism," *American Prospect* (January 24, 2012), http://www.the-american-interest.com/articles/2012/01/24/the-once-and-future-liberalism.

8. "Quick Facts about Nonprofits," http://nccs.urban.org/statistics/quickfacts.cfm.

9. "Fact about American Religion," http://hirr.hartsem.edu/research/fastfacts/fast_facts.html#attend.

their peak in 1970, and not many today provide the active, face-to-face involvement in community affairs and civic engagement that has traditionally made them schools of self-government and citizen autonomy.[10] Yet compared globally, US civil society is still robust, and still offers opportunities for citizens to exercise political power and push back against the encroaching power of the state.

The rise of the Tea Party movement in 2009 illustrates the possibilities provided by civil society. Like-minded citizens angry over high taxes, increasing deficits, excessive government spending, the bailouts of banks and the mortgage industry, and greater government intrusion into the economy began to organize themselves in order to put political pressure on their members of Congress and work to elect representatives who shared their concerns. Technologies like the Internet and cable news made it possible for this amorphous, scattered, localized discontent to quickly connect with others, publicize their concerns across the country, and coalesce into a national organization. A rant against government bailouts on the floor of the Chicago Mercantile Exchange by a CNBC business news editor on February 19 was the spark that lit this political tinder, but the accelerant was a video that went viral after it appeared on the Drudge Report, which is visited by nearly two million people a day. Overnight, local and national Tea Party websites were created, and within a few months hundreds of nationwide protest rallies were held. The movement played a big role in shifting the majority in the House of Representatives to the Republicans in 2010, with the Tea Party Caucus in the house comprising sixty-two Republicans in 2011.

The Tea Party has faded somewhat, but still remains a potent political force in national politics, whether for good or ill, depending on one's political point of view. But the rise of the Tea Party shows that the traditional dangers of democracy such as accountability to the voters, and the new technologies that exacerbate old fears such as demagogues enflaming the masses, can also be instruments for citizens unhappy with the intrusive power of the federal government to organize resistance and effect change.

––––––––––

10. See data in *Bowling Alone* (New York, 2000), 438–39.

Finally, the First Amendment guarantee of free and open speech still remains in force. The explosion of raucous protests at various "town hall" meetings held by members of Congress with their constituents in August 2009, most directed against the proposed Affordable Care Act, was a rare moment in US politics of direct confrontations between citizens and their representatives, many of whom would be voted out of office in 2010. Moreover, many of these confrontations were filmed and ended up on YouTube, publicizing the events nationally and illustrating once again how the numerous blogs, websites, social networks, and online magazines have expanded the exercise of the right to political speech to millions of people. Ordinary citizens now can potentially reach a national audience once reserved for the few-score columnists, network news anchors, and magazine writers that three decades ago monopolized and controlled political opinion. Whatever the dangers of this expansion of what antidemocrats like Socrates or Fisher Ames would have considered uninformed opinion arising out of the irrational passions and ignorance of the masses, the existence of these venues for exercising free speech and reaching a large audience offers as well an opportunity for mobilizing resistance to the federal Leviathan.

Most important, millions of people in the United States still possess the qualities of independence, self-reliance, resistance to tyranny, and love of freedom that have always characterized the American character. Millions from all walks of life have not yet changed into the "innumerable multitude of men, all equal and alike, incessantly endeavoring to procure the petty and paltry pleasures with which they glut their lives," as Tocqueville described the denizens of soft despotism. Like Benjamin Constant, they want government authorities "to keep within their limits" and "confine themselves to being just," and prefer to "assume the responsibility of being happy" for themselves. And like C. S. Lewis, they rankle at the patronizing arrogance of a government increasingly taking responsibility for their lives and well-being at the cost of their autonomy. They still see such "kindness" as an "intolerable insult" that puts them on "a level of those who have not yet reached the age of reason or those who never will" and "classed with infants, imbeciles, and domestic animals." In short, millions of people in the United States of all races and conditions still prefer to stand on their own two feet, to take responsibility for their own lives, and to pursue their happiness according to their own lights. All they ask is to be left alone.

The continuing vigor of the US Constitution and the US character both give us hope that democracy's dangers and discontents do not have to end in soft despotism, and that we can restore the limited government of the founders and recover US democracy's "aptitude and strength."

BIBLIOGRAPHY

Adams, Henry, and Ernest Samuels. *History of the United States of America During the Administrations of Jefferson and Madison*. Chicago: University of Chicago Press, 1967.

Adams, John. *The Works of John Adams, Second President of the United States*. Edited by Charles Francis Adams. Boston: Little, Brown and Company, 1851.

Aeschylus. *Aeschylus I*. Translated by H. Weir Smith. Cambridge, MA, and London: Harvard University Press, 1922.

Ames, Fisher. *Works of Fisher Ames with a Selection from His Speeches and Correspondence*. Edited by Seth Ames. Boston: B. Franklin, 1971.

Aristophanes. *Aristophanes I: Acharnians, Knights*. Translated by Jeffrey Henderson. Cambridge, MA, and London: Harvard University Press, 1998.

———. *Aristophanes II: Clouds. Wasps. Peace*. Translated by Jeffrey Henderson. Cambridge, MA, and London: Harvard University Press, 1998.

Aristotle. *The Complete Works of Aristotle*. Edited by Jonathan Barnes. Princeton, NJ: Princeton University Press, 1984.

Athenaeus. *The Deipnosophists*. Translated by Charles Burton Gulick. London: W. Heinemann, 1927.

Bailyn, Bernard, ed. *The Debate on the Constitution*. New York: The Library of America, 1993.

———. *The Ideological Origins of the American Revolution*. Cambridge, MA: Harvard University Press, 1967,

Borning, Bernard C. *The Political and Social Thought of Charles A. Beard*. Westport, CT: Greenwood Press, 1984.

Bowling, Kenneth R., and Donald R. Kennon, eds. *Inventing Congress: Origins and Establishment of the First Federal Congress*. Athens: Ohio University Press, 1999.

Carey, George W., and James McClellan, eds. *The Federalist*. Dubuque, IA: Kendall/Hunt Publishing Company, 1990.

Churchill, Winston S. *The Gathering Storm*. New York: Mariner Books, 1985.

Cicero, Marcus Tullius. *The Orations of Marcus Tullius Cicero*. Translated by C. D. Yonge. Covent Garden: George Bell and Sons, 1856.

Demosthenes. *Demosthenes. Orations*. Translated by J. H. Vince. Cambridge, MA, and London: Harvard University Press, 1930.

Eberstadt, Nicholas. *A Nation of Takers: America's Entitlement Epidemic*. West Conshohocken, PA: Templeton Press, 2012.

Eisenach, Eldon J., ed. *The Social and Political Thought of American Progressivism*. Indianapolis: Hackett Publishing Company, 2006.

Euripides. *Euripides IV*. Translated by David Grene, Richmond Lattimore, and Frank William Jones. Chicago: University of Chicago Press, 1968.

Farrand, Max, ed. *The Records of the Federal Convention of 1787*. New Haven, CT: Yale University Press, 1937.

Ferguson, Niall. *The Great Degeneration: How Institutions Decay and Economies Die*. New York: Penguin Press, 2012.

Finley, M. I. *Democracy Ancient and Modern*. New Brunswick, NJ: Rutgers University Press, 1985.

Foner, Philip S., ed. *The Democratic-Republican Societies, 1790–1800: a documentary sourcebook of constitutions, declarations, addresses, resolutions, and toasts*. Westport, CT: Greenwood Press, 1976.

Goldberg, Jonah. *Liberal Fascism: The Secret History of the American Left, from Mussolini to the Politics of Change*. New York: Three Rivers Press, 2007.

Hansen, M. H. *The Athenian Democracy in the Age of Demosthenes*. Berkeley and Los Angeles: University of California Press, 1991.

Hayek, F. A., and Ronald Hamowy. *The Constitution of Liberty*. Chicago: The University of Chicago Press, 2011.

Herodotus. *The Histories*. Translated by Robin Waterfield. Oxford and New York: Oxford University Press, 1998.

Isocrates. *Isocrates II*. Translated by George Norlin. Cambridge, MA, and London: Harvard University Press, 1929.

Jones, A. H. M. *Athenian Democracy*. Baltimore: Johns Hopkins University Press, 1986.

Kagan, Donald. *The Great Dialogue: History of Greek Political Thought from Homer to Polybius*. New York: Free Press, 1965.

Kalb, James. *The Tyranny of Liberalism: Understanding and Overcoming Administered Freedom, Inquisitorial Tolerance, and Equality by Command*. Wilmington, DE: ISI Books, 2008.

Kennan, George Frost. *The Cloud of Danger: Current Realities of American Foreign Policy*. Boston: Little, Brown, 1977.

Kurlantzick, Joshua. *Democracy in Retreat. The Revolt of the Middle Class and the Worldwide Decline of Representative Government*. New Haven, CT, and London: Yale University Press, 2013.

Jefferson, Thomas. *Writings*. Edited by Merrill D. Peterson. New York: Library of America, 1984.

Lattimore, Richmond. *Greek Lyrics*. Chicago: University of Chicago Press, 1960.

Lefer, David. *The Founding Conservatives: How a Group of Unsung Heroes Saved the American Revolution*. New York: Sentinel, 2013.

Lewis, C. S. *God in the Dock*. Grand Rapids, MI: William B. Erdmans Publishing Co., 1970.

Lincoln, Abraham. *The Collected Works of Abraham Lincoln*. Edited by Roy Basler. New Brunswick, NJ: Rutgers University Press, 1953.

Lippmann, Walter. *Liberty and the News*. New York: Harcourt, Brace and Howe, 1920.

Lovejoy, Arthur O. *Reflections on Human Nature*. Baltimore: Johns Hopkins University Press, 1961.

Lysias. *Lysias*. Translated by W. R. M. Lamb. Cambridge, MA: Harvard University Press, 1930.

MacDowell, Douglas N. *Aristophanes and Athens*. Oxford: Oxford University Press, 1995.

Mahoney, Daniel J. *The Conservative Foundations of the Liberal Order: Defending Democracy Against Its Modern Enemies and Immoderate Friends*. Wilmington, DE: ISI Books, 2010.

Main, Jackson Turner. *The Antifederalists: Critics of the Constitution, 1781–1788*. New York: Norton, 1974.

Mandelbaum, Michael. *Democracy's Good Name. The Rise and Risks of the World's Most Popular Form of Government*. New York: Public Affairs, 2007.

Manent, Pierre, and Paul Seaton. *Democracy without Nations? The Fate of Self-Government in Europe*. Wilmington, DE: ISI Books, 2007.

McClelland, J. S. *The Crowd and the Mob from Plato to Canetti*. London: Unwin Hyman, 1989.

McDonald, Forrest. *Novus Ordo Seclorum: The Intellectual Origins of the Constitution*. Lawrence: University Press of Kansas, 1985.

McDougall, Walter A. *Freedom Just Around the Corner: A New American History, 1585–1828*. New York: HarperCollins Publishers, 2004.

Minogue, Kenneth. *The Servile Mind: How Democracy Erodes the Moral Life.* New York: Encounter Books, 2010.

Moreno, Paul D. *The American State from the Civil War to the New Deal: The Twilight of Constitutionalism and the Triumph of Progressivism.* Cambridge: Cambridge University Press, 2013.

Nisbet, Robert. *The Present Age: Progress and Anarchy in Modern America.* Indianapolis: Liberty Fund, 1988.

Oates, Whitney J., and Eugene O'Neill Jr. eds. *The Complete Greek Drama: All the Extant Tragedies of Aeschylus, Sophocles and Euripides, and the Comedies of Aristophanes and Menander, in a Variety of Translations.* New York: Random House, 1938.

Osborne, Robin. *The Old Oligarch. Pseudo-Xenophon's Constitution of the Athenians.* Kingston upon Thames: London Association of Classical Teachers Occasional Research Series, 2004.

Ostwald, Martin. *From Popular Sovereignty to the Sovereignty of Law: Law, Society, and Politics in Fifth-century Athens.* Berkeley: University of California Press, 1986.

Payne, George Henry, ed. *The Birth of the New Party or Progressive Democracy.* Naperville, IL: J.L. Nichols, 1912.

Pestritto, Ronald J., and William J. Atto, eds. *American Progressivism.* Lanham, MD: Lexington Books, 2008.

Pindar. *The Odes of Pindar.* Translated by Richmond Lattimore. Chicago: University of Chicago Press, 1947.

Plato. *The Dialogues of Plato.* Translated by Benjamin Jowett. New York: Random House, 1937.

———. *Plato I. Euthyphro, Apology, Crito, Phaedo, Phaedrus.* Translated by Harold North Fowler. Cambridge, MA: Harvard University Press, 1914.

———. *Plato: Laws Books 1–6.* Translated by R. G. Bury. Cambridge, MA: Harvard University Press, 1926.

Plutarch. *Plutarch Lives.* Translated by Bernadotte Perrin. Cambridge, MA, and London: W. Heinemann, 1914.

Polybius. *The Histories.* Translated by Ian Scott-Kilvert. Harmondsworth, England: Penguin Press, 1979.

Putnam, Robert D. *Bowling Alone: The Collapse and Revival of American Community.* New York: Simon and Schuster, 2000.

Rahe, Paul A. *Republics Ancient and Modern, Volume 1: The Ancien Régime in Classical Greece.* Chapel Hill: University of North Carolina Press, 1994.

———. *Republics Ancient and Modern, Volume 2: New Modes and New Orders in Early Modern Political Thought.* Chapel Hill: University of North Carolina Press, 1994.

———. *Republics Ancient and Modern, Volume 3: Inventions of Prudence: Constituting the American Regime*. Chapel Hill: University of North Carolina Press, 1994.

———. *Soft Despotism, Democracy's Drift: Montesquieu, Rousseau, Tocqueville, and the Modern Prospect*. New Haven, CT: Yale University Press, 2009.

Remini, Robert V. *The Legacy of Andrew Jackson: Essays on Democracy, Indian Removal, and Slavery*. Baton Rouge: Louisiana State University Press, 1988.

Richard, Carl J. *The Founders and the Classics: Greece, Rome, and the American Enlightenment*. Cambridge, MA: Harvard University Press, 1994.

Richardson, James D., ed. *A Compilation of the Messages and Papers of the Presidents*. New York: Bureau of national literature, inc., 1897.

Roberts, Jennifer Tolbert. *Athens on Trial: The Antidemocratic Tradition in Western Thought*. Princeton, NJ: Princeton University Press. 1994.

Roosevelt, Theodore. *The Autobiography of Theodore Roosevelt*. Edited by Wayne Andrews. New York: Scribners, 1958.

Rossum, Ralph A. *Federalism, The Supreme Court, and the Seventeenth Amendment: The Irony of Constitutional Democracy*. Lanham, MD: Lexington Books, 2001.

Samons, Loren. *What's Wrong with Democracy? From Athenian Practice to American Worship*. Berkeley and Los Angeles: University of California Press, 2004.

Scott, James C. *Two Cheers for Anarchism: Six Easy Pieces on Autonomy, Dignity, and Meaningful Work and Play*. Princeton, NJ: Princeton University Press, 2012.

Shrimpton, Gordon S. *Theopompus the Historian*. Montreal and Kingston: McGill-Queen's University Press, 1991.

Somin, Ilya. *Democracy and Political Ignorance: Why Smaller Government is Smarter*. Stanford: Stanford University Press, 2013.

Stockton, David. *The Classical Athenian Democracy*. Oxford: Oxford University Press, 1990.

Thucydides. *The Landmark Thucydides: A Comprehensive Guide to the Peloponnesian War*. Edited by Robert B. Strassler. Translated by Richaard Crawley. New York: Free Press, 1996.

Tocqueville, Alexis de. *Democracy in America*. Edited by Philip Bradley. Revised by Frances Bowen. New York: Alfred K. Knopf, 1994.

Voegeli, William. *Never Enough: America's Limitless Welfare State*. New York: Encounter Books, 2012.

Washington, George. *The Papers of George Washington*. Edited by Dorothy Twohig and W. W. Abbot. Charlottesville: University Press of Virginia, 1983.

Weissberg, Robert. *Polling, Policy, and Public Opinion: The Case Against Heeding the Voice of the People.* New York: Palgrave Macmillan, 2002.

Wilentz, Sean. *The Rise of American Democracy: Jefferson to Lincoln.* New York: Norton, 2005.

Williamson, Chilton. *American Suffrage from Property to Democracy: 1760–1860.* Princeton, NJ: Princeton University Press, 1960.

Wood, Gordon S. *The Creation of the American Republic: 1776–1787.* Chapel Hill and London: University of North Carolina Press, 1998.

Xenophon. *Xenophon I. Memorabilia, Oeconomicus, Symposium, Apology.* Translated by E. C. Marchant and O. J. Todd. Cambridge, MA: Harvard University Press, 1923.

ABOUT THE AUTHOR

BRUCE S. THORNTON grew up on a cattle ranch in Fresno County, California. He received his BA in Latin in 1975 and his PhD in comparative literature in 1983, both from the University of California at Los Angeles. Thornton is currently a professor of classics and humanities at California State University in Fresno. He has authored nine books and more than four hundred essays, columns, and reviews on classical culture and its influence on contemporary political and educational issues. He is a research fellow at the Hoover Institution at Stanford University and a member of Hoover's Working Group on the Role of Military History in Contemporary Conflict.

**WORKING GROUP ON THE ROLE OF MILITARY
HISTORY IN CONTEMPORARY CONFLICT**

THE WORKING GROUP ON THE ROLE OF MILITARY HISTORY IN CONTEMPORARY CONFLICT has set its agenda mindful of the Hoover Institution's dedication to historical research in light of contemporary challenges and, in particular, reinvigorating the national study of military history to foster and enhance our national security.

Chaired by Hoover senior fellow Victor Davis Hanson with counsel from Hoover research fellows Bruce Thornton and David Berkey, along with collaboration from the group's distinguished scholars, military historians, security analysts, journalists, and military veterans and practitioners, this team examines how knowledge of past military operations can influence contemporary public policy decisions concerning current conflicts. The careful study of military history offers a way to analyze modern war and peace that is often underappreciated in this age of technological determinism. The result of such study is an in-depth and dispassionate understanding of contemporary wars, one that explains how particular military successes and failures of the past can be often germane, sometimes misunderstood, or occasionally irrelevant in the context of the present.

INDEX